"With a storyteller's rhythmic cadences, the narrative chronicles the adventures of Anpao as he persists in his arduous quest for the love of the beautiful Ko-ko-mik-e-is. Because the oral tradition upon which Anpao's adventures are based includes many diverse elements, the book may be perceived as a unique blending of history and mysticism. [It is] a magnificent, long-needed achievement."

—*The Horn Book*

"Highwater spins his tale with the lyric cloth common to myths and legends. He views Anpao as 'an Indian "Ulysses"' whose odyssey will help illuminate 'the Indian concept of nature and man's place in the cosmos.' Clearly in this he has succeeded."   —*The Boston Globe*

"The book ANPAO is aimed at young adults but it is a delightful reading experience for people of all ages."

—*The San Francisco Examiner*

Also by Jamake Highwater

———◆———

THE CEREMONY OF INNOCENCE

I WEAR THE MORNING STAR

LEGEND DAYS

MANY SMOKES, MANY MOONS:
*A Chronology of American Indian History
Through Indian Art*

ANPAO

An American Indian Odyssey

Jamake Highwater

Pictures by

Fritz Scholder

HarperCollins*Publishers*

"Anpao and Coyote" (pages 249–251) is reprinted from Melville Jacobs, *Northwest Sahaptin Texts* (1934), by permission of Columbia University Press.

Anpao: An American Indian Odyssey

Text copyright © 1977 by Jamake Highwater

Illustrations copyright © 1977 by J. B. Lippincott Company

Library of Congress Cataloging-in-Publication Data

Highwater, Jamake.

Anpao.

Bibliography: p.

SUMMARY: Traditional tales from North American Indian tribes woven into one story that relates the adventures of one boy as he grows to manhood.

I. Indians of North America—Legends. [1. Indians of North America—Legends] I. Scholder, Fritz, birth date II. Title.

E98.F6H58   398.2′097   77-9264

ISBN 0-397-31750-6

ISBN 0-06-440437-4 (pbk.)

First Harper Trophy edition, 1992.

18 LSCH 22 21

For

Virginia and Frederick Dorr

and Frances Grigsby

———————

The giving earth remembers
and only men forget.
The animals and man have lost
their little dreams
and have awakened together.

John Neihardt, *Black Elk Speaks*

Contents

————◆————

I   In the Days of the Plentiful   11

II   The Dawn of the World   45

III   The Lessons of Heaven and Earth   85

IV   The Invasion from the Sea   181

The Storyteller's Farewell   239

Notes on Sources   247

Bibliography   253

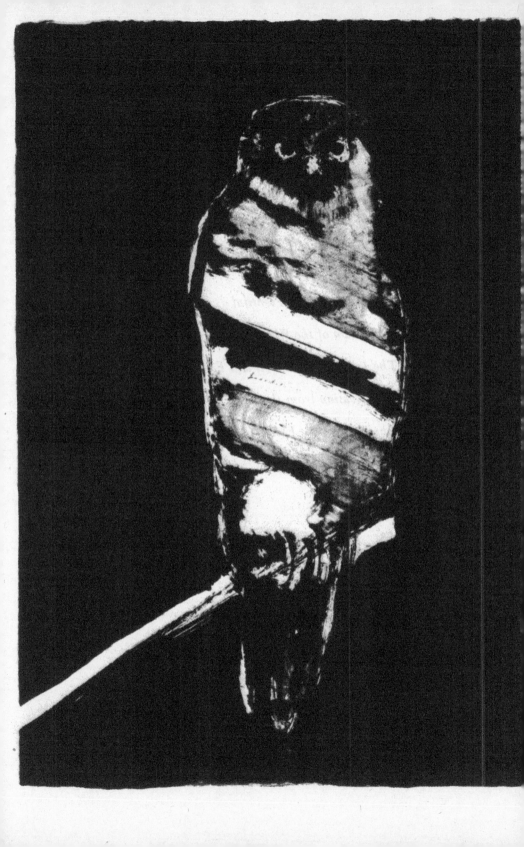

I

In The Days of the Plentiful

Ah, I Shall Tell

The holy man Wasicong sat by the lake in the night, luminous in the light that rose from the water as he listened to the distant drums and to the singing.

"Ah," he said. "Do you hear the voices of the children? And do you hear the voices of the women laughing?"

And then he pointed down into the moon-filled water where shimmering images of liquid-people in the drowned village at the bottom of the lake rose like smoke on a clear night.

"Can you hear their singing?" he said.

> The world is dangerous
> ...dangerous for Indians.
> Come with me, my people,
> and I will show you the way to safety.
> Here, under the water...here
> is a magical place.
> Here is the place created by him
> to keep his people safe forever.

And then old Wasicong looked up into the perfect moon and smiled slowly and rustled his cloak of feathers.

"Ah," he said. "I shall tell you a story of how the world began and how the boy Anpao was born and of his adventures among the people and among the spirits." And he winked his large yellow eye and nodded.

"Ah," he hooted softly. "I shall tell you if you will come near and look into my face. Ah . . ." Wasicong whispered as he leaped into the air effortlessly and flew to the top of a pine tree.

"Ah," he hooted at the moon, "I shall tell."

In the Days of the Plentiful

I n the days before the people fled into the water, the wind held leaves aloft in the sky like dragonflies. There was no war and people were at peace. The buffalo-people lived in the world of the sweet grass below, and the sky above was filled with birds of many colors and of many songs. The air was blue and the earth was green and each thing rested upon the other. In the forest the leaves fell slowly. There was no fear. The birds did not leap into flight when the cats awoke. And the wild flowers changed colors to amuse themselves.

Anpao and his twin brother Oapna had spent many years traveling through the great world in search of their destiny. One winter they came upon a village high in the mountains. The people who lived there invited them to spend the cold days in comfort. The young brothers accepted gladly, for they were poor and hungry. They had searched long and hard for wisdom and vision without success.

A very beautiful girl lived in the village. When a young man looked upon her, the world would stop. Music would beat in his blood and he could see one hundred white deer sleeping in the sun-blanched meadow of her forehead. She was more beautiful than flowers, more eloquent than antelope, and very proud. All the young men wanted to marry her, but whenever they tried to speak to her about love, she said she did not want a husband. She was so beautiful that young men were made miserable if they looked upon her face.

"How is this, Ko-ko-mik-e-is?" asked the young men. "Why do you not want to marry? How is this, Ko-ko-mik-e-is, that you will not speak to us? We are rich and handsome fellows and many of us are brave and daring."

But Ko-ko-mik-e-is only laughed at them. "Why should I marry?" she replied. "My father is rich. Our lodge is good. We have plenty of food and tanned robes and soft furs for winter. So what good is a husband?"

Anpao and his brother laughed at the young men who were forever trying to attract the attention of the beautiful Ko-ko-mik-e-is. When the Raven People held a dance, the young men put on their most splendid ornaments and each tried to dance with greater elegance than the next. But when they asked Ko-ko-mik-e-is if she would come and sit with them, she laughed and went into her lodge and would not come out. "I want no husband," she said.

Then the Bulls, the Kit-Foxes, and many of the other clans held their dances. The young men who were rich and those who were great among their people tried to win the attention of Ko-ko-mik-e-is. The strong and handsome asked for Ko-ko-mik-e-is.

"No," she called from within her lodge. "I want no husband."

"Ho!" her disgruntled father exclaimed, for he was

getting angry with his daughter. "Why do you refuse these men who call to you? You have been asked by our best young men and you say always the same, No! No! I am unhappy with you, Ko-ko-mik-e-is. I begin to think that maybe you have a secret boy friend!"

While the father of Ko-ko-mik-e-is was shouting, Anpao and his brother Oapna crept to the lodge entrance and waited there in hope of getting some food. But the argument continued and they were afraid to interfere.

"Please," Ko-ko-mik-e-is was pleading, "do not be angry. I have no lover, Father, and I have done nothing with anyone. It is the great Above Person . . . it was he who told me that I must not marry any of these young men. He has told me that I belong to him alone. He is the great person called the Sun. He said to me, *Be careful, Ko-ko-mik-e-is, and listen to me because I have great power. You must not marry. You are mine. . . .* That is what he told me," she said, and wept.

Anpao and Oapna looked at each other in amazement. "Do you think it is true that this beautiful girl is promised to the Sun?" Anpao whispered.

"No, I do not believe it," said Oapna. But, being Contrary and therefore always doing and saying everything backward, he really meant, Yes, I do believe it!

"I am sad, brother," Anpao said, and sighed. "I too love this beautiful Ko-ko-mik-e-is. But if she wants the Sun and if she rejects all these rich boys, what chance do I have?" And Oapna shook his head no in agreement.

Anpao and Oapna were strangers in the village. They

had no father and they did not know their mother. They had nothing, not even memories of the land of their people. Though they were handsome young men, their clothes were so shabby that they felt miserable and shy beside the beautifully dressed youths of the village. And though they were tall and strong, each had a mysterious scar upon his face.

"Ko-ko-mik-e-is would surely be insulted if we asked to marry her," Anpao murmured sadly.

"Ah," Oapna said. "It is hopeful."

"Yes," Anpao agreed. "It is hopeless."

The celebration was almost over, and the young men of the village were angry because Ko-ko-mik-e-is had rejected all of them once again. They grumbled to one another and danced furiously.

Then one of them noticed the brothers sitting at the door of the lodge of Ko-ko-mik-e-is. He laughed bitterly and said, "Ho! Why don't you ask her to marry you? You are so rich and handsome she will surely accept you!"

The other boys jeered and pranced around the brothers. Soon everyone had come to laugh at them, but Anpao and Oapna did not laugh. Oapna slowly got up and smiled to show his great anger.

"Yes!" Oapna said. "We are very rich. Yes, we will do exactly what you have said. I will go and ask her to marry me!"

The people laughed, for they didn't realize that Oapna was Contrary and therefore meant exactly the opposite of what he was saying. Now even the old people were making fun of the brothers. Anpao could tolerate it no longer. He stood up with great pride and indignation and brushed the dust from his shabby clothes. This made the people laugh all the harder. Only Ko-ko-mik-e-is, from within her lodge, looked on with sympathy.

Anpao walked resolutely to the river and waited there at the place where the women came to draw water. Soon the beautiful Ko-ko-mik-e-is approached. "Psssst," Oapna called to his brother, but Anpao paid no attention to him and waited anxiously as Ko-ko-mik-e-is came toward him. He took a breath and tried desperately to think of something noble to say, but facing the beautiful girl was more difficult than any ordeal he'd ever confronted. Fearing that if he hesitated any longer Ko-ko-mik-e-is might leave, Anpao said the first thing that came into his head, "Wait!"

At the sound of his twin's voice, Oapna was seized with embarrassment and hid in the bushes and covered his head. But Ko-ko-mik-e-is did not laugh. And she did not run away. She looked at Anpao and waited for him to speak.

The first word, difficult as it had been, was far easier than all the rest. Anpao was so nervous he could barely breathe. Slowly the villagers surrounded them and became utterly silent, waiting for Anpao to speak.

"I want..." said Anpao. "I want to speak to you, Ko-ko-mik-e-is." And suddenly a wonderful nobility overtook the wretched-looking boy, and from somewhere within his shabby exterior came the voice of an eloquent man.

"I want to speak to you honestly and openly where all the people can hear me," he said.

"You speak well," Ko-ko-mik-e-is said softly. "I will listen to you."

"I have spent many days in your village. And I have

seen you refuse all the young men, though they are rich and brave and handsome. Now, today, these men have laughed at my brother and me and said, Why do you not ask for her? They laugh at us because we are poor. We have no lodge, no food, no furs, no splendid ornaments or robes. We have no family, no memories. We are alone. But we are noble—for everything in the world is noble—and we are proud, because everything in the world can be proud. These young men are rich in the riches of their fathers, but we are rich in the riches of the earth. These young men have hidden under the shadows of their mothers, while we have journeyed through the world in search of our own wisdom. We are not yet wise, but we are seeking wisdom. We are not willing to barter for it or to inherit it. So now you know us, beautiful Ko-ko-mik-e-is. We ask you to take pity on one of us and to be his wife."

Everyone waited anxiously in the silence to hear what Ko-ko-mik-e-is would say to Anpao. Even Oapna took courage and crept out from the bushes so he could hear the reply.

"It is true," Ko-ko-mik-e-is said, "that I have refused all the rich young men. Now you have asked for me and I am glad. Yes, I will be your wife, Anpao, and my people will be happy. You are poor, but poverty does not matter. My people will give you dogs. My mother will make us a fine lodge. My father will give us furs and robes for winter. You will be my husband and your brother will be my brother."

Anpao and Oapna were stunned with delight. They tried to embrace Ko-ko-mik-e-is, but she held them away and said, "Wait! The Sun has asked for me. He says that I may not marry, that I belong to him. But now I say, go to the Sun. Tell him: *She whom you spoke with believes your words. She has never loved anyone. But today she wants to marry Anpao.* You alone can find the Sun because you are brave and adventurous. You must tell him that you want me for your wife. Then you must ask him to take the scars from your faces. That will be his sign to me. I will know he is pleased and will not punish me. But if he refuses, or if you fail to find his lodge, then you must never return to my village and I will never marry."

"Ah!" Anpao exclaimed. "At first your words were good and I was glad. When you spoke to us I was happier than I have ever been. But now I cannot smile because of the task you have given us to perform. Where is the lodge of the Sun? Where is the trail that leads to it? Which path must be followed? Does anyone know? Has any person ever journeyed to the lodge of the Sun?"

Then Ko-ko-mik-e-is covered her face and backed away. "I am afraid, Anpao," she whispered. "I am afraid of the Sun. I will wait for you, but you must do what I have asked. You must get the consent of the Sun or I cannot marry." Then tears came to her eyes and she hurried into the lodge and would not come out again.

Anpao and Oapna sat down and covered their heads with their robes and tried to think what to do.

"We must not find someone who will help us," Oapna said after thinking for a long time.

"You are right," agreed Anpao. "Let's go talk to the

old woman who gives us food. Perhaps she will help us."

When they found the woman, Anpao hesitantly tapped her arm. "Pity us," he said. "We are very poor and we must go away on a long journey. Old woman, we have no Grandmother Spider to help us. Please make us some moccasins or we shall never be able to travel to the end of the world."

"But where are you going?" the old woman asked. "There is no war; our lives are peaceful. You should stay here where there is food and fire and friends."

"No, we cannot stay. We must go."

The woman looked into the boys' faces and, seeing that they spoke the truth, she nodded thoughtfully. "Then it is so," she murmured sadly. And she sat within her lodge and made the twins many pairs of moccasins with strong hide soles. When she had finished, she called the boys to her and wished them good fortune. She gave them a sack of food —pemmican of berries, pounded meat, and dried back fat.

"You must do what you must do," she said to them, as they waved farewell and walked slowly toward the trees beyond the village.

With only each other for company, the twins were sad as they climbed the slopes surrounding the village of Ko-ko-mik-e-is. After many hours they finally reached the summit of the pine-covered mountain, and they paused to take a last look at the little village below. Anpao wondered if he would ever see Ko-ko-mik-e-is again.

"*Hai-yu!* Pity us, Sun," he prayed, and together the boys turned and started into the vast, rugged canyon where no person had ever ventured before.

The Magic of the Moon

For many days the brothers traveled over great prairies, through precipitous canyons in which the water leaped, along wooded ridges, and among grass-rich valleys. Every day their sack of food got lighter and the twins were fearful that they might starve. Their poor robes became poorer. Their moccasins were battered by the sharp rocks, and their leggings were torn by the thorny tangle of the land without trails. At night the wind hissed its disregard for their shabby robes.

"Wind," Anpao chanted in a feeble voice in the hope of giving his brother courage, "you sing in a loud voice today. The land stretches far before me, before me stretches far away."

Oapna was not listening. He had not spoken for many days and he did not take his head from under his robe.

"Wind's house is thundering," Anpao chanted at the top of his voice. But still his brother would not respond. "Wind's house is thundering around us. It goes roaring over the land, the land covered with thunder. Over the windy mountains, over the hills, and among the rocks comes the wind on many legs. The wind comes running toward us. The

Blacksnake-Wind comes to me, comes and wraps itself about me, comes here running with its thunderous song."

Then Anpao became silent.

Just when he was about to confess to his brother that their journey was too hard and they must abandon their quest, Anpao saw an old man in a coat of wolf fur peeking out at them from behind the trees. "*Hai-yak!*" he called to the man.

At the sound of Anpao's voice the man disappeared into the bushes, but after a moment he cautiously peeked out and his ears stood up alertly. He sniffed the air carefully and then, satisfied that the strangers were not evil, he slowly approached them.

"What are you doing here, boy-people?" he asked in a soft, husky voice. "What are you doing so far from the place of your people?"

"Ah," sighed Anpao. "We are looking for the place where the Sun lives. We have been sent to speak to him," Anpao explained as Oapna sank to the earth in exhaustion and hunger. The man in the wolf coat sniffed Oapna cautiously, until he was convinced that the boy was not a dangerous person despite the fact that he was covered entirely by his robe.

"Ah," said the old man, sitting down and scratching himself with his foot. "I know all this land—all the prairies, and the mountains, and even the great desert in the South— but I have never seen the house of the Sun." Then he thought for a moment. "But," he said, "at a certain time the Earth opens in the West, where its mouth is. It is the place

from which, long ago, the wolves came. The Earth opened
and they came out of its mouth and settled here. But the
Earth became angry and ate up the wolf-children. The
wolves were frightened and so they ran away, moving farther
West. They journeyed toward the sunset, leaving me here
alone."

The old man tilted his head far back and howled sadly.
"Ah," he said. "They may know the Sun, but I do not know
him and it is unlikely that I ever will. But I know someone
who may tell you. There is someone beyond here—the
striped-face. She is very wise. Go and ask her." Without another word, the old man pulled his fur tightly around him
and scampered into the forest, barking madly as he went.

"*Hai-yu! Hai-yu!*"

The cry came from behind the twins. Both of them
jumped to their feet, and Oapna poked his head out from
beneath his robe for the first time in days.

"Who is that not?" he shouted. "If you are not, I
will!"

"What is the matter, little brothers?" an old lady whispered as she came out of the water and pulled her long hair
back to reveal her beautifully striped face. "I would be your
friend if you could be less violent."

"Forgive us," Anpao said. "My brother and I are hungry
and tired. We did not see you and your voice frightened us."

"Perhaps I can help you," said the old lady, as she sat
by the edge of the water and carefully washed the food she
had collected.

"Please take pity on us. Our food is gone, our moccasins are worn out, and now we will die."

"What is it, my poor boy-people? Tell me and perhaps I can help you."

"The girl I wish to marry belongs to the Sun."

"Ah, that is very sad indeed," the old woman said, without glancing up from her work.

"We are trying to find where he lives."

"Ah!" The little striped-face lady smiled. "I know where he lives. But now it is nearly night. You must rest and I will share my food with you. Tomorrow I will show you the trail to the big water. It is very far away, but that is where the Sun lives, on the other side of the water."

After Anpao and Oapna had eaten they felt much stronger. They relaxed for a long time by the fire and watched the dance of the flames. Immediately after dinner the little striped-face lady had scurried back into the water to collect twigs and sticks for the elaborate dam she was building across the river. She chattered happily to herself as she worked. Now and again she scampered onto the river bank and shook the water from her long hair and, standing tall on her little legs, inspected her work with great pride.

The brothers offered to help with her project, but the striped-face one laughed as she splashed back into the river. "This is not work for boy-people," she said. "You must save your strength for your long journey to the Sun."

The brothers grew tired of watching the fire. So they decided to explore the hill behind their camp. At the top was a vast, grassy place where stars sometimes fell from the sky and flew like insects toward the earth. It was a wonderful place to play.

"Look, Oapna!" Anpao shouted. "The Moon is very beautiful tonight!"

"No, it is very ugly!" Oapna agreed.

"Oh, you must be careful when you talk to the Moon. She may not understand that you are Contrary and your words could make her angry, Oapna."

But Oapna was so enthralled by the glorious light of the great white globe that danced in the black sky, he simply could not be silent.

"It is the ugliest thing I have ever seen!" he shouted. "It is so little and so dark. I think I have never seen the Moon looking so ugly!"

"Be careful, Oapna," his brother begged. "You must not talk that way to the Moon!"

Suddenly the night became very dark and Anpao trembled. He could see a ring of light taking shape around them.

"Help!" someone cried out in the darkness.

Anpao reached to embrace his brother but could not find him. Then the ring of light vanished and Anpao discovered that he was alone. He called to Oapna for a long time but there was no reply. The grass on the beautiful hill had turned black as if a fire had raged in the darkness. The night was now moonless and there was no sound except the distant splashing of the old striped-face woman in the river. He called to his brother again, but still there was no reply. He looked everywhere but there was no sign of Oapna.

Then gradually the Moon reappeared. And next to it

was a very bright new star. Anpao sat on the hill and stared up at the Moon and the star. "I think I will try to shoot down that star next to the Moon. It is so beautiful that I would like to capture it and take it home to Ko-ko-mik-e-is." So he stood up and aimed his arrow at the glistening star. Pulling as far back on his powerful bow as he dared, he shot into the sky. Then he sat down, exhausted, to watch. "Ah!" he exclaimed, when the star dimmed.

He leaped to his feet again and began to shoot arrow after arrow at the star. So powerful was his bow that not a single arrow fell back to the earth. Gradually the star faded, and at last it fell.

As Anpao watched it plummet to earth, a terrible feeling swept over him. He looked into the sky and it was empty. Now there was only a great, leafless tree at the summit of the hill. He could see something hanging limply from its branches. At first Anpao was afraid to approach the tree, but his curiosity was so great that he overcame his fear and slowly began to climb toward the top of the black hill. As he crept toward the tree the air became thin and the stars burned so near and so brightly that he could not look into their glistening light. He covered his head with his robe and staggered toward the summit where immense flashes of flame burst and fell to the ground like sparks from an angry bonfire. The thunder roared and the wind galloped on hoofs of stone across the scorched hilltop.

Anpao fearfully approached the thing that was dangling from the black tree. For a moment he could not move, but he summoned all of his courage and hesitantly reached out to touch the thing hanging there.

It was cold. And soft. And wet. It was a person hanging there by the legs. The head was swinging ever so gently in the wind.

Anpao wanted to run away, but he could not take his eyes off the swaying body. Slowly he drew the head toward him so he could see if it had a face.

"Ah!" he cried as the lightning flashed, for he could see poor Oapna's features in the burst of light. "Ah!" he screamed, pulling his hand away and staring at his blood-stained palm. "AH!" he howled, and he fell back and stumbled, staggering to his feet and hurtling blindly down the hill, yelling as he ran away from the horrible sight. Falling against the stinging trees as he plunged into the forest. Collapsing at the edge of the boiling river. Trying to call for help. But the night glowed with fierce, cold moonlight. And then the darkness came.

"*Kyi!*" Anpao shouted when he awakened. All he could see was two little gray eyes in a striped face. "*Kyi!*"

When he sat up, he realized that the eyes were those of the old striped-face woman. She smiled at him strangely and tickled his face with the gleaming feather of a raven.

"And do you know what has happened to you and do you believe what has happened to you and do you want me to tell you more?" she taunted softly.

"No," Anpao said as he pushed the old woman away and stood up. "I do not believe any of this!"

"Ah." She chuckled and shook her head. "That is good and that is not so good."

"I'm hungry and I have hurt my hand. Look at it. It is

bleeding. You must help me, old striped-face. Please."

"Ah," she whispered, wiping the blood from Anpao's hand. "There, you see, it is gone."

Anpao was amazed. He stared at his palm, for there was no wound. "But what have you done to the wound?" he exclaimed.

The old woman chuckled again and wrinkled her striped nose as she scampered around Anpao. "It is not *your* wound, brotherless boy. It is not *your* blood." Then she stopped and leered at him. "Ah," she growled softly. "What have you done with your brother? Ha!" she shouted as she ran to and fro, looking under rocks and into bushes. "He is not here! And he is not there! Ah!" She groaned softly, coming up very close and staring into Anpao's face with her little gray eyes. "What have you done with your brother-brother-brother?"

"It was his own fault!" Anpao exclaimed. "He is Contrary! He is always making trouble!"

"Ah-ha!" The old woman laughed loudly. "I like him! He is a smart one, that Contrary boy!"

"It was his own fault," Anpao repeated meekly. "I warned him."

But the old woman wasn't paying any attention. She grinned maliciously and put her tongue between her lips and peered at Anpao with her cold little eyes. "Who are you?" she whispered in a small, shrill voice. "Who are you, boy?"

"I am Anpao!" he said proudly.

"Oapna? Did I hear you say Oapna? Ah!" She giggled as she scurried around him, flapping her arms so that the fur on the back of her cloak bristled. "Where is you? Is you who? Ah-ha! Anpao? No, Oapna! Yes, no, yes...ah-ha!"

Then she shouted and showed her ferocious teeth. "Do you think I am stupid?" she hissed into his face. "Do you think I do not know who you are and how you came to have a Contrary brother? Do you think I am just a little creature who knows nothing but how to build dams of sticks?"

Anpao backed away from the angry old woman, but she followed closely after him. Then she suddenly smiled. "You are a *good* boy," she purred. Anpao was relieved that her anger had passed. "Ha!" she shouted so abruptly that he fell down. She crawled over his chest and put her face up against his face.

"I do not like *good* boys," she snarled. "Without your brother you are only half a boy!" She shook her head and smiled. "Ah," she moaned as she got up and stumbled toward the water, puffing like someone who had run a very great distance. "Ah," she wheezed laboriously, as the air seemed to come from her mouth in a stream and she began to get smaller and smaller. "Ah," she sighed pathetically as she reached the edge of the river and slipped silently into the dark water. "Anpao, you must find yourself," she gurgled softly as she vanished.

Anpao mourned the loss of his poor brother. Lying beneath the gloating Moon, he could not sleep. He wanted to continue his search for the Sun so he could receive permission to marry Ko-ko-mik-e-is, but he could not abandon Oapna. He was certain that the Moon had taken his brother.

She often stole people who she felt had insulted her. She was haughty and would not permit anyone to be disrespectful. Of all the things in the world the Moon was the coldest, and the one whose favor was most difficult to obtain. Looking up into the white face of the Moon, Anpao tried to think of how he could reclaim Oapna. But the Moon went behind a dense cloud that covered her face. In the darkness Anpao became sleepy. Despite his concern for Oapna, he could not fight his fatigue and gradually he dozed off.

When he awoke his head felt heavy and it was difficult for him to stand. Vines and grass had grown over him while he slept. He seized a berry bush that was tangled in his hair and pulled it out. It was loaded with ripe berries. After Anpao had eaten most of the fruit, he carefully twisted the branch back into his long hair and immediately he felt much strengthened. So he started the long journey back up the terrible hill on which Oapna had vanished. About noon he again felt hungry and, pulling the branch from his hair, he found that it was now loaded with blue huckleberries. On the sky-high hill it had become summer.

By the time Anpao reached the top he was exhausted. He gathered soft brush and moss and lay down to sleep on the shore of a vast lake that stretched into the sky. While he slept, a person came to him and shook him gently, saying, "Get up—I have come for you."

Anpao awoke with a start and looked around, but he saw no one. Then he rolled over and pretended to go back to sleep. He waited for a long time and then through the corner of his eye he saw something approaching. It was a very small person wearing the bright white skin of a swan. Anpao could not decide whether this creature was a girl-person or a swan-person. He remained very still until it reached out to shake him again.

"Ha!" shouted Anpao, leaping up and grasping the long neck of the creature. "I have you now! Who are you and what do you want? Tell me or I will throw you into the lake and drown you!"

"I do not care," the creature screeched. "Throw me into the lake!"

Anpao was so angry that he threw the creature into the water with all his strength. There was a great splash. When the water settled Anpao saw that the bright white person was laughing at him as she gracefully glided back and forth in the water.

"Foolish boy," she said, "you are too fast to be wise and too slow to be clever." Anpao tried to reach her, but could not. "I have come for you. My grandmother has sent me to bring you to her house. If you will act kindly, I will try to help you. Come, slide onto my back and I will take you to my grandmother."

At first Anpao did not trust her, but her voice was agreeable and there was no malice in her laugh. She waved her long graceful arms and beckoned him to the water's edge, where she helped him sit on her gleaming white cloak of feathers. Soon they were gliding swiftly across the great water toward the land of the Moon.

They reached a tiny island on which there was nothing but a single little house. The white girl told Anpao to leap ashore. Then she laughed and ducked under the water, leaving him there quite alone.

"Kah," he heard someone cackle at his side. When he turned he saw an old gray woman standing there. "What is it you have come in search of, my boy-son?"

"Excuse me," Anpao gasped in surprise.

"Tell me, what can I do to help you? Indeed you seem much in need of help. You cannot swim across the lake by yourself, and you cannot fly through the sky. Your poor legs are much too small to carry you swiftly, and your little arms are too short to help your legs to run faster. My-my-my," she clucked with deep concern. "You are not made very well, my poor featherless friend. But tell me, what kind of person are you and how can I help you?"

"It is my brother, Oapna," Anpao exclaimed. "He was stolen by the Moon when she was in a rage."

"My-my-my," the old woman clucked again. "The Moon is always in a rage. Ever since the day her husband the Sun took a handsome young woman for his mistress, the moon has been angry," the old woman complained. "She is always happy to punish anybody who remotely resembles that girl-person the Sun loved. And I must confess, you do very much resemble that unfortunate woman."

"But my brother and I did not intend to offend the Moon," Anpao said. "You see, my brother is Contrary—when he says one thing he means the opposite. He was only praising the Moon in his own way. So why won't she leave us alone? After all, we cannot help it if the Sun fell in love with an Earth-woman!"

"Ah," clucked the old woman, waddling around and pecking among the leaves that had washed onto the strand of her tiny island. "That does not matter, my flightless friend. The girl friend of the Sun did not like living in the sky. No, indeed. She tried to escape and return to her people. But unfortunately for her she did not succeed."

"Well, if she did not succeed, why is the Moon so angry?"

"Ah," sighed the old woman, squatting comfortably among the leaves. "No one understands the Moon. She has no reasons—only wishes. And what she now wishes is to have the child. You see, there was a child. The Sun had a child with the girl, and the Moon is forever frightening children in the hope that one of them is the child the Sun gave to his mistress."

"I do not care at all about the problems of the Moon," Anpao exclaimed impatiently. "I only care about my brother. And I want to get him back!"

"That will not be easy," the old woman said sadly. "The Moon is feared by everyone. From all others we can run away, but from her there is no escape. She strikes and there you lie —dead. You should forget about your brother. Turn back! Go home! Would you dare enter the lodge of the Moon?"

"I have seen the Moon and I do not fear her!"

"You have seen her from afar, but you have not seen her true face," the old woman whispered. "So do not be foolish," she said sternly. "The ordeal that awaits you is the most terrible possible. The lodge of the Moon is made of white stone. It is a fierce and terrible place. Hanging everywhere within her lodge are eyes—yes, the eyes of those she has stolen! She has taken out their shining eyes and hung them in her lodge. Now, then, do you dare go to such a place as that?"

"I will tell you honestly, old woman, I am afraid." And Anpao covered his face, as he realized that he might have to abandon his brother.

"It is true," he murmured, "that I am afraid. I cannot roar or leap high into the air. I do not have great teeth or powerful talons. I have no wings or quills. I am just a naked fellow with a thin brown skin that is easily broken. So I must tell you honestly—I am afraid. But I cannot go away. I cannot run away and hide. There is something else that I possess. My talons are in here, old woman—they are in my head. And my wings, do you see, they are also inside me. Here in my breast. I am afraid, but still I will go where everyone else is afraid to go. Because these wings upon which we poor naked brown people fly will not let us rest. They beat frantically within us. And my talons reach out toward whatever remains unseen, toward whatever remains un-known. I will tell you honestly, old woman, I am much afraid, but fear is not enough to stop me. As long as there is life within me there will always be the frantic flapping of my wings, carrying me toward those impossible things that have not yet turned upon the world."

The old woman looked at Anpao with great compassion and slowly nodded her head.

"I see that you must do this impossible thing, so perhaps I can help you," she said. "No one has ever looked at the dreadful lodge of the Moon and lived. It is the dark side of the Moon, the one she hides from us. When she lives with her husband the Sun, she is a different person. But when she is in her lodge, everyone fears her. There is but one creature whom the Moon fears. And that person is I, the old woman with the skin of the white swan. That is why my people and I came to live on this island so close to the lodge of the Moon. We alone are safe from her anger. Now, my little nude-person, I will give you powerful medicine and help you to regain your brother. I have heard the boy crying every day. He is in the Moon's lodge, but she has not yet eaten him. For that you should be glad. But he screams and cries day and night."

"Oh, take pity on me and help me, and I promise I will honor your people all my life!"

"Yes, I will help you. But first you must eat, for you will need all your energy." The old woman put her hand to her mouth, and berries appeared in her palm. After giving him the berries, she put her hand to her mouth and produced meat. Then she gave Anpao a spruce cone, a rosebush, a piece of devil's club, and a small piece of whetstone to take with him. "These things will save you," she whispered.

"Why do you deceive me?" Anpao cried. "My heart is sad. I am crying. My brother is gone and you wish to make a fool of me." And he covered his head with his robe and wept.

"Ah," said the old swan-woman. "You do not believe in me. Come out, come out from under your robe. I will make you believe, foolish featherless-boy."

Anpao uncovered his head and followed the old woman to the edge of the water.

"Do you see what I have here?" she asked. She took a strange object from her cloak of feathers. "It is a pipe. Do you see? Here is the bowl that I have carved of sacred stone and here is the staff that I have carved of sacred wood. I will give you this pipe and you will see how powerful it is."

But Anpao did not believe the old woman, and he refused to take the strange object from her.

"Do you wish to save your brother?" she asked him, waddling into the water and beginning to glide away.

"Yes! Yes!" shouted Anpao. "Please do not go away! I will do what you say!"

"Then come and take this pipe from me," she said, and laughed.

"But I cannot. I cannot swim in this great water. It is too deep and too dark."

"Cannot...cannot...is there anything you *can* do? Come, do as I tell you. Come into the water!" Reluctantly Anpao walked toward the old woman who extended the pipe to him. He held his breath as he reached the water's edge, afraid that this too could be a trick of the Moon to drown him. Then a most amazing thing happened. As he stepped toward the old woman, the water seemed to recede little by little, just in front of his feet. Finally he grasped the pipe and held it tightly in his hands. He felt great power flow into him.

"Now you will believe me," said the the old woman. "Take what I have given you and go and find your brother. But do not forget who helped you or how you and your people came to have this powerful medicine pipe!"

Anpao thanked the old woman and returned to the

shore. There three swans took him upon their backs and glided across the great water toward the lodge of the Moon.

When Anpao arrived at the darkest, farthest shore of the great water, he could hear his brother screaming with pain. Soon he could see the lodge of the Moon, bursting with light so bright that Anpao could not look at it. He covered his eyes with the rosebush the old woman had given him and carefully worked his way toward the dazzling house.

He knew that he would be caught if he tried to enter the opening in the lodge, so he silently climbed to the top and peeked down through the smoke hole. What he saw was terrifying. Walls made of white stone blazed like ten thousand fires. Thunder sat in a black cloak in one corner of the lodge, while Lightning sat in another. The Moon stood like white fire in the middle of the chamber, bristling with furious cold and looking around with luminous, terrible eyes. Surrounding her were countless pairs of bobbing eyes which watched in utter terror but could not escape the sinews from which they were dangling.

Oapna was hanging by his arms from the smoke hole above the terrible blast of heat and cold that rose from the Moon and her friends. Each time Thunder roared and Lightning flashed, the lodge seemed to catch fire and Oapna screamed in fear. Each time he screamed, they laughed. He had hung from the top of the lodge for so long that his fingers were bleeding, but he would not let go, for he knew that if he fell he would be eaten at once and only his eyes would remain.

Just as the Moon reached toward Oapna with her freezing fingers, Anpao remembered the power of his medicine pipe and quickly reached down through the smoke hole and pulled his brother to safety. "Oapna, I have come to save you!" he shouted, as he dropped the spruce cone into the lodge, telling it to make the outcries of his brother. Then they scrambled off the roof and began to run faster than they had ever run before.

The Moon and her terrible friends were not fooled by the screams of the spruce cone. They realized at once that their captive had escaped. So the Moon quickly drew her molten robes around her shoulders and started in pursuit. When Anpao saw her leap into the sky, he threw down the piece of devil's club, and where it landed a great patch of devil's club arose. The Moon had great difficulty getting through the tangle. Soon, however, she was close behind them again. Anpao threw the rosebush to the ground, and a vast thicket of roses grew in the path of the Moon. But at a single wave of her arm the roses withered. When the Moon approached the brothers once again, they threw the whetstone on the earth, and it became an enormous cliff. The Moon could not climb it without getting hopelessly tangled in her long glistening robes.

At last Anpao and Oapna reached the water's edge where the swans anxiously awaited them. The brothers leaped upon the swans' backs and in a moment were safely across the water. When they looked back they saw the Moon standing at the top of the great cliff, shouting abuse at them.

The boys reached the old woman's house and found her waiting for them. She gave them food and they sat happily among the feathered-people and celebrated their reunion. When all the food had been eaten and the people had settled under their feathered cloaks and the fire had become low, the old woman began to chant:

"This prayer I offer you:
May your road be fulfilled
reaching to the house of your Sun father.
When your road is fulfilled,
in your thoughts may we live.
May we be the ones whom your thoughts embrace.
On this day,
to our Sun father,
we offer prayer meal.
To this end:
May you help us all to finish our roads well."

When the old woman finished her song, she smiled at the brothers and asked them if they knew where they had come from.

"Yes, of course," said Anpao. "We come from the village of Ko-ko-mik-e-is."

This answer made the old woman laugh softly.

"But it is true," Anpao insisted.

"Ah, yes, my son, but I was not asking from what village, but from what mother, you have come."

"Ah," Anpao sighed. "That is something we do not know. We lost our parents so long ago that we do not recall our mother or our father."

"And tell me, my sons, would you like to remember what you have forgotten?"

"Oh yes!" Anpao exclaimed.

"Oh no!" Oapna agreed.

"Then I will help you. But in order to remember you must do something for me. You must sing the first song you learned to sing."

"Ah," Anpao muttered, "let me try to think. That is very difficult. I am not certain I remember."

The old woman waited patiently while the brothers whispered to each other and tried to recall the first song they ever learned. While they searched their memories, the old woman stirred the fire. In the yellow glow that arose, the brothers' memories glowed with new light. And in the darkness around the fire they could see that many many others had come to join their encampment. The newcomers formed a large circle beyond the firelight.

"Perhaps you should ask the help of the pipe," the old woman said, as the brothers gazed at the people who sat huddled in their fur and feather coats.

And so, for the first time, the pipe was lighted and under the new stars it was passed around the great circle of all the people of the land. The fire arose and the drums began to sing. Anpao stood up very slowly and opened his arms to the night. Then he began to sing:

> "My mother bore me,
>> ah,
> within a raincloud,
>> ah,
> that I might weep with rain,
>> ah,
> that I might whirl with the cloud."

It was the first song of Anpao.

"Now," whispered the old woman, "sit down, my sons, and listen very carefully, for I shall tell you a story—of how the world began and how the boy Anpao was born and of his adventures among the people and among the spirits. I shall tell you everything if you will come close and look into my face. Ah, my sons, I shall tell."

II

The Dawn of the World

The Dawn of the World

At the place where all things began, there was first the black world. And Old Man, the all-spirit, lived in this void, silently and without motion. For he was he.

The all-spirit was also her and all that exists between the her and the him, like the snail which from itself brings new life. For Old Man was without mother or father, being together something and nothing.

He looked around him, but there was nothing but himself to see. He listened carefully, but there was only silence. Nothing was born and nothing grew. Nothing was new and nothing old. There was only Old Man, alone in an unthinkable forever.

Because he was everything, Old Man was not lonely. But as he radiated through the endless time of nothingness, it seemed to him that something might be more interesting than nothing. Here and there within his immensity were specks of his power.

So he drew himself inward like a vast breath. And all that he was came together in one place, like the place in the acorn which imagines the tree. There he glowed with power until suddenly he was ignited by an idea of being. And from this mysterious center of the all-spirit came a light into the blankness which was so great that it illuminated all that had been in darkness, reaching beyond the farthest specks of him that is called everything.

First came white—of the brightness of him.

Then he made a great water filled to its depths with all that he knew. And from the sea could come all life that ever would be, so deep and so rich was that great water which Old Man had made.

Then came green—of the waters of him.

Because Old Man was each thing and also everything, he could feel the coolness of the water and he could taste on his lips the salt from it. And just as he was thinking that this water which he had made was good, his thoughts shattered by accident and broke into fragments which fell through him and into the water. From this dazzling shower of bright yellow thoughts came the beings of the water, first so small that they could scarcely be called anything at all and then larger, until the fish, swimming in the deep, appeared one at a time. And then the snails and crawfish, the mussels, and the grass that grew beneath the water.

And blue was the sky where the water and the light mingled. And brown and russet and black the creatures in the sea he had made.

"Hmm," said Old Man. "I am forever, but still I grow older and older. Since I have made so beautiful a reflection of myself on this green water, perhaps I should also make something that will continue to live on the surface of the water when my reflection has gone. For I also created youth and old age when I created time." And so it happened. Now there were snow geese and mallards and teal and coots and terns and loons, living and swimming about on the water's surface. Old Man could hear the splashing of their feet and the flapping of their wings.

Then the snow goose paddled to where she believed Old Man was, and she said, "I do not see you, but I know you are within me and outside of me everywhere. Listen to me, Old Man. This is very good water that you have made. But birds are not like fish. Sometimes we get tired of swimming around. Sometimes we would like to get out of the water."

"Then fly!" Old Man rejoiced, and he waved his arms so that a wind came and all the water birds flew, skittering along the surface of the deep green sea until they moved fast enough to soar into the air.

And the sky was dark with them and full of their clatter.

"How beautiful these flying birds are, and what a good idea that they should fly!" said Old Man.

The loon was the first to glide back to the surface of the water. "Old Man," he said—looking all around, for he knew that Old Man was everywhere around and within him —"Old Man, you have made us a fine sky and bright light in which to fly, and you have made us water to swim in, but still, though it must sound ungrateful to want more, there is something we need. When we are tired of swimming and also tired of flying, we should like a dry place where we can walk around and sleep. Old Man, give us a place to build our nests, please, and we will make many blue and white and speckled eggs for you to look at!"

"Well," Old Man said slowly, "that is not too easy. To make such a place, I must have your help. By myself, I have already made four difficult things: the green water, the white light, and the blue sky, not to mention the people of the water. Now I must have help if I am to create more, for I am very old and cannot do it by myself."

"We will help!" exclaimed all the water-people. "We are ready to do what you say!"

Old Man stretched out his hands and beckoned. "Let the fastest and also the biggest of you try to help me find land," he said.

"I am ready to try," the snow goose said, and she drove herself along the water until the wake behind her grew to a point that drove her up high into the air. She flew into the sky until she was no more than a speck against the bright light. Then she turned and, plummeting down like an arrow, dived into the water.

Down, down, down she went, into the deep green water until she could not be seen—not even by the eyes of Old Man. She was gone a very long time. Old Man counted slowly to four hundred four times before she rose to the surface of the water, where she gasped for air.

"What have you found?" Old Man asked her.

"Nothing. I have brought nothing," the goose said sadly.

Then the loon tried, and after him, the mallard. Each bird flew high into the sky and then turned and dived down,

down, into the water. And then each rose wearily from the depths and murmured, "Nothing," when Old Man asked what had been found.

And Old Man shook his head and sighed. Only the little coot was left. He paddled busily in the water, dipping his head under the surface and making his happy gibberish.

"Old Man," the little coot whispered, "when I dip my head into the green water I think that I see something there, very, very far below in the dark. I am small, I know, but perhaps I can swim deep enough to reach it. I cannot fly high into the sky, nor can I dive like my brothers and sisters; I can only swim. But I will try my best to swim deep into the water and find what we are looking for. May I try, Old Man?"

"Little brother coot, I have asked for help, and certainly every one of the water-people is welcome to try. It is possible that what those who can fly and those who can dive cannot accomplish, the coot, who can only swim, may yet achieve. Try, little brother, and see how well you can do."

"Ah-ho!" the little coot exclaimed. "Thank you, Old Man!" And he tipped smoothly under the water and swam down, down, and farther down into the deepest green of the green water, until at last he was out of sight.

Little coot was under the water a very long time, longer than any of his brothers or sisters. Just as Old Man and the other water-people were afraid that he had vanished forever, a very small dark spot appeared far beneath the water's surface, but none of them could see what it was. The tiny spot rose and rose until at last Old Man and the birds saw that it was the little coot, desperately swimming up from the very bottom of the salty green water in which everything that would ever be already was.

The coot splashed to the surface and stretched his neck for breath, but he would not open his beak to gasp for air.

"Ah, give me what you have brought, little coot," Old Man said, holding his hand under the coot's beak. A small ball of mud fell into his palm. "Thank you, little brother, for what you have brought."

Then Old Man looked at the bit of mud and he smiled and began to roll it slowly in his hands. Then he smiled once again. And the ball of mud grew and grew until even Old Man could not hold it. So he looked around for a good place to put this muddy world, but there was only water and air, for nothing else yet existed.

"Come, brothers and sisters, you must help me again, for I must find a place for this land which you have asked me to create for you." All the people of the water came to Old Man, and he tried to find among them the right creature to carry the large ball of mud. But the mussels and the snails and the crawfish were too small, and they lived much too deep in the water to keep the island afloat. And the fish were too narrow. No, the fish would never do. And when Old Man looked around for someone else to carry the land which he had created, he saw that only one water-person was left. "Ah, Grandmother Turtle," he said, "you are very slow, but you are strong and perhaps you can help me."

Grandmother Turtle feebly swam to Old Man and waited patiently while he piled the mud on her back and made a shape of it which completely covered her. "Ah," said Old Man, "we have done it!"

Now there were earth and water and there was the great blue sky. But on the Earth there was nothing.

Old Man looked around and shook his head. There seemed always to be something else that needed to be created.

"Our beautiful Earth should be fruitful," said Old Man. "Let it begin to bear life!"

When Old Man said this, trees and grass and flowers sprang up to become the fragrant hair of the Earth. The flowers rose upon her hills, and the fruits and the seeds glowed in the Sun and blew perfume into the wind. The many birds of the sky came to sleep in her palms when they were tired, and the fish came close to her side to nibble the tender roots.

Old Man said, "Ah," and smiled as he looked at Earth, for she was very beautiful—truly the most beautiful thing he had made so far. "The Earth should not be alone," Old Man thought. "I shall give her something of myself so she will know that I am near and that I love her dearly."

And Old Man reached into himself and from his body he pulled out a rib and breathed upon it, then laid it softly on the Earth. The bone moved slightly and then gradually it came to life and it stood up and walked upon the Earth. And so it was that people were made.

As the days passed, and the Moon rose and circled the Earth, and the Sun glowed and set, the children of these first people were born. And they wandered over the Earth and ate of her fruitfulness and were born into many generations, until at last all the animals had come from them, as well as all the men and women of the Earth.

The animals heard and knew Old Man, and all the birds of the air heard and knew him also. All things that he had made loved him and understood him when he spoke to them—the birds, the animals, and also the people.

The years passed and Old Man became older and older. As he traveled around the sweet Earth, the animals would help him climb the mountains, and the birds would flutter around his head to cool his brow. Snakes led him safely through the jungle, where the spiders wove a glistening hammock for him to sleep in.

The moons came, one after the other, and Old Man grew still older. One day he was traveling about, making people as he went, making stones and turquoise and silver as he stumbled along. He busied himself making the mountains, the prairies, the forests, the deserts, and the redwoods, which he blessed with very long life and with branches that reached into the bluest of the blue sky. So he went along, humming merrily and making things as he went: putting rivers here, and waterfalls there, putting red paint and brown paint here and there into the hills, and tossing armfuls of snow upon the tips of the great mountains. And he smiled and said, "Ah, it is better to make something than to do nothing. It is better to be something than to be nothing. It is better to know than not to know. It is better to be than not to be." Then he continued on his way, covering the plains with tall grass for the animal-people to eat, putting roses on the rosebushes and ferny tops on the orange spikes he pressed into the Earth to make carrots. While he was in the prairie, he made the big-horn and let it go free. But it tripped and fell down and did not seem able to manage in the tall grass. So Old Man impatiently took it by one of its horns and led it up into the mountains and turned it loose there. Immediately it skipped away, stepping easily from rock to rock and going up terrifying slopes where other animals would not venture. Then he said, "I can see, Bighorn, that this place suits you well. Stay here and be happy."

While Old Man was in the mountains, he made the antelope and turned it loose, to see what it would do. It ran so fast that it constantly fell over rocks and hurt itself. Old Man knew that this would not do, so he took the antelope down to the prairie and set it free. It ran off as gracefully and as fast as a bird in the sky, and Old Man smiled and said, "Ah, no matter how great you are, you must be willing to make a few mistakes if you would be the kind of person who creates new things."

One day Old Man came upon a river and found a woman and a man standing there watching the dead leaves floating past in the swift current.

"How is it, Old Man?" the woman asked. "Will we always live; will there be no end to it?"

Old Man said, "I have never thought of that. We will have to try to decide it now. I tell you what, I will throw this chip of wood into the water. If it floats, people will die, but they will die for only four days, after which time they will come back to life." When he threw the chip into the river, it floated, and Old Man smiled.

But the woman seemed displeased. "No," she said, "I will throw this stone into the river. If it floats, we will always live, and if it sinks, then we must die forever." Before Old Man could stop her, the woman had thrown the stone into the river, where it immediately sank to the bottom.

"Ah," said Old Man. "My daughter, you have chosen death. Now there must be an end to all the people of Earth."

And Old Man walked away sadly, nodding his head.

A few nights later the woman's only child died in its sleep, and she cried out and threw her body on the ground. "Oh! Old Man, listen to me, please! I did not know that death would be so terrible. Let us change this to the way it was first when the chip of wood floated on the water!" she said, and wept.

But Old Man sighed and said, "Not so. What you have done is done. We can undo nothing that we have done. The child is dead; therefore people will have to die. Even I must grow old. Nothing is permanent and nothing can remain unchanged and something must become nothing as it was in the beginning."

And Old Man went into the mountains to get away from the terrible sorrow of the woman. He tried to sleep, but his bones were too old and his breath was too short, and before the dawn, Old Man began to sink into nothing just as the stone had sunk into the water of the river.

"I do not wish to leave these things which I have made. I do not wish to leave the sight of the beautiful Earth and all her people, or of the sky and the river and the sea. But I must go." And he smiled and nodded his head.

"Gentle . . . gentle, little coot, dig a bed for Old Man so he can sleep with Earth about him. And before I sleep, I will create one last thing so that women who weep for the dead will also be happy. From such women will come children who hunger for the stars and who will climb the mountains to be close to them. From such women will come creatures of so vast a hunger that they will raise themselves in spirit until they fly above death in the memories of all their people."

And Old Man fell to his knees in the newly turned soil of the Earth and, as the first light of the new day came into the sky, a great river began to flow from him and he was gradually covered by the water. His last word came from his watery mouth as his hand reached to take the glowing Sun into his palm.

"*Anpao!*" he whispered. "It is the dawn of the world!"

And he was gone.

Anpao Is Born

——————

O nce again the sacred pipe was lighted and, under the new stars and among all the people of the land, it was passed around the great circle where the twins sat with the old swan-woman. The campfire rose into delicately twisting flames and the drums sang.

The old woman smiled with satisfaction. "I have told you the story of how the world began. But that is just the beginning of the story. Now a new day has come. Do you see the Sun that begins to awaken in the East?"

Anpao stood up slowly and opened his arms to the sky. He felt as if he were floating in the misty light of dawn. He had to concentrate in order to keep his toes touching the ground.

Oapna had fallen asleep while the old woman told her story, and he lay wrapped in a blanket of swan feathers. But even in his sleep he seemed to ebb and drift in the new light of the Sun.

The old woman chuckled quietly as she laid more branches on the fire and glanced at Anpao. "You are confused. But that is as it should be. Did you know that your name has a special meaning among the people who live high upon the prairie? And do you remember what your name means?"

Anpao nodded his head dreamily, trying to focus on the old woman who faded away and then gradually came back again. As she spoke she crept close and pressed her little face to his.

"Ah," she murmured so softly that he could barely hear what she was saying, "the *dawn*! That is what Old Man said, is it not? And that is who you are, foolish boy!" And suddenly she cackled loudly and ran wildly around the astonished youth.

"*Anpao, An-PAY-oh!* It is the dawn! It is the dawn! Ha, you do not know. You do not know your name and you do not know how the world began, and I do not think that you even know where you came from!"

The old woman continued to cackle to herself as she raced around and around Anpao so quickly that he could see only a blur.

"Now!" yelped the old woman, stopping abruptly and staring at Anpao. "Listen carefully! Watch me carefully—every movement! You are coming under the power of the great medicine of the pipe, my boy-person; that is what is happening to you. So watch *everything*. For this is your dream, Anpao. It is your dream alone, and no one else can dream your dream and no one else can remember it. Listen carefully, Anpao, for I shall tell *everything*. I shall whisper many secrets in your ear. Listen!" she murmured, as she slid soundlessly to the brink of the roaring fire and smiled with blazing little eyes, stepping gradually into the twisting orange flames and tilting her head to the side as she smiled blissfully.

"*Ah*," she purred, as flames came from her mouth like

words, "*ahhhh-yes-my-little-boy-person.* Can you feel it now? You are tinier than the tiniest of things. Anpao is a child-seed, a tiny seed and nothing more. Anpao, can you feel it? Anpao is being born. He is the tiniest of tiny things. Take care and remember this well, Anpao, for you will not be born again!"

Then she pointed her flaming fingers toward the sky, where the mouth of the earth was open and a great emanation of light poured ceaselessly into the dissolving night.

"It was a sad time. The woman whose only child had died wept when she saw the dawn," the old woman was chanting softly into the fire. "Listen," she murmured. "I shall tell . . ."

Each day the woman wept and each day she longed for her child. But she could not find Old Man to plead with him, and she would not sit at her loom and weave, or sing songs for her husband, so great was her misery at the loss of her child.

On the morning that Old Man vanished into the earth, the woman wandered out of her village by the river and walked aimlessly into the light of the dawn, hoping to find Old Man and recover her child from death.

She walked all day and she walked all the next day and the day after that. Each morning she found that she was no closer to the dawn than she had been the day before. No matter how far she walked, or how many mountains she climbed, the dawn always evaded her. Finally, just when she was about to give up and return unhappily to her village, she stopped by a lake and saw in the water that she had become old and ugly from her grief.

So she sat by the lake and combed her hair and put ornaments of shell and stone around her neck, and slowly the old age retreated from her face and she was beautiful again. At that moment, the Sun, who was dawning, caught sight of this beautiful woman and fell in love with her. The woman could feel the warmth of the Sun on her shoulders when he smiled at her, and, with renewed hope of finding Old Man, she stood up and started again toward the dawn.

Whereas previously the woman had vainly run toward the dawn without being able to touch it, today she could easily get a footing in the rays of sunlight. And so she began to run upward into the sky toward the dawn.

It was in this way that the woman went up to the World-Above-the-World without dying. She went up while she was still alive and very beautiful, and she met the Sun and stayed with him and had a new child, whom she named Anpao.

The woman, the Sun, and Anpao lived in seclusion so that the Moon, who was the first wife of the Sun, would not discover that her husband had taken a human wife. They lived in the world that is behind the clouds, so far away that people see only its blue floor which is the luminous roof of the earth.

One day the Sun went to his old mother and asked her, "My mother, will you make my mistress a tipi? She is a young woman, and she should have a tipi of her own, but she does not know how to make one." His mother agreed and made a handsome white tipi, painted with images of her son's proud deeds. This the Sun asked of his mother so the woman would not be lonely for her village or her husband or her lost child. And so the couple and their child, Anpao, lived happily in the beautiful tipi in the World-Above-the-World. And for a time the Moon knew nothing of it.

Each morning the Sun awoke and washed his face with the clouds of the night which, as they dissolved into water, made the sky turn very blue and clear. While he washed, his human wife made breakfast. After eating, the Sun took up his bow and his quiver of arrows and went out into the sky to hunt for food for his family.

"What are you going to do today?" the Sun asked as he was leaving the white tipi one morning.

"I think," answered his mistress, "that I will dig some roots. If you shine brightly for me, it will make the day nice and the wild potatoes will ripen quickly. I think I will take my digging stick and go to gather some wild potatoes."

"Yes," the Sun agreed. "And I will bring back some deer meat. And when you go to dig for potatoes," asked the Sun, "will you take Anpao with you or leave him here with my mother?"

"Oh!" the woman exclaimed. "I would not go anywhere without my Anpao!"

"Good," said the Sun. "But there is one thing you must remember, and you must also tell little Anpao to remember —neither of you should ever forget it. Do not dig up a wild potato if the top has been eaten off."

The woman laughed. "But why?"

"Because it will bring misfortune. And that is all I know of it." Then the Sun left the tipi.

The woman and her boy wandered on foot all the day. She showed him how to use the digging stick, and by dusk their skin sack was filled with wild potatoes. The Sun had kept his promise and brought a fat deer, which the wife cooked with the potatoes. And in the night, while the tipi glowed from the light of their fire, the family had a fine dinner. Afterward, the Sun lighted his pipe of carved stone and told stories of Old Man, who had created everything.

When the morning came, the Sun again prepared to go hunting after breakfast. "Are you going to gather potatoes again today?" he asked.

"Yes. They are ripe and I want to dig enough so I can dry some for the winter when the ground is cold and nothing grows."

"That is good, but always remember what I told you: do not dig a potato from which the top has been eaten."

"Yes, yes, yes," the wife said impatiently. "I will remember. I will not forget."

The woman and her son, Anpao, spent the entire day collecting wild potatoes. As she walked, bent over from the large sack of potatoes on her back, she saw a large potato plant just beside the path. Its top had been partially eaten. "Ah-ha," she muttered to Anpao. "Perhaps a powerful creature the Sun fears has eaten the top off that potato. I had better not dig it." But instead of continuing toward her tipi, the woman lingered, looking down at the potato and wondering why it should be forbidden to dig it. "I will dig it!" she said aloud. "It will just fill my sack. After all, what can it hurt?"

So the woman knelt with her digging stick and tried to pry the plant from the ground. It was a difficult task, and at first the plant would not budge. But suddenly it came free, and the woman fell back and stared in amazement at the hole she had made in the ground of the World-Above-the-World. Instead of a hollow of soil where her digging stick had turned the potato over, there was a large round hole filled with sky. Trembling and clutching her son to her, she bent forward to peer through the hole.

She gasped and leaped to her feet in fear. There, far below, she could see the entire earth whirling in its mantle of clouds. The great water of salt was there just as the Old Man had made it. There were the rippling prairies of grass, the willows and poplars which grew along the winding rivers. What an amazing sight for the woman to see: the immense jagged rocks of the mountains and the boiling springs and geysers; the great river of white water, and the redwoods, which had grown almost to touch the World-Above-the-World since the woman had last seen them when she was a child on earth. She could even see the camp of her people where happy women played with their children.

"Oh!" the woman exclaimed in anger. "That is why the Sun did not want me to dig a potato from which the top had been eaten! He is jealous and was afraid that I would grow lonely if I saw my village!"

And indeed the sight made her very sad.

For a long time the woman sat quietly beside the hole in the sky, watching her people and crying with loneliness for them. When finally it began to get dark and the woman knew that her husband was on his way home, she took the forbidden potato plant and resealed the hole which she had made and hurried to the tipi, hoping she would arrive before the Sun did.

When the Sun came home, the woman told him nothing about the hole she had made in the sky.

Each day, after that, when the Sun went hunting, his wife would slip away to the place where she had made the hole. She would pull up the potato plant and peep through and watch her own human people. It was autumn in the world far below, so the people there were drying meat and preparing sinew, which the women would use to stitch the winter moccasins.

The mistress of the Sun was preparing sinew too. But she did not intend to make moccasins. Soon she had a coil of sinew so large that she had to hide it under her bedding, where her husband would not discover it. Each day she braided the sinew into a long rope. And each day she hid it under her bedding.

Whenever the Sun came home, the woman and child were in their tipi, ready for dinner. The Sun never saw his mistress do anything wrong. She kept faith with him as far as he knew and it did not occur to him to distrust her.

But during each day, when the Sun was away, the woman went to the place where she had made the hole and lowered the rope through it in order to see if it was long enough to reach all the way down to the earth. Little by little it spanned the great distance between sky and earth.

Finally the day came when the rope of sinew was almost long enough to touch the ground below. The woman was very happy as she searched the forest near the hole for a root strong enough to hold her weight. Finally she found a very strong root and tied the rope to it, hiding it under the leaves. Then she put the potato plant back into the hole and hurried home, carrying Anpao on her back.

The Sun reached the tipi first that night, and when his mistress came home he looked at her sternly. "Where have you been? And why have you stayed away so late?"

"I have been gathering wood for the fire," she said. But the Sun looked at her suspiciously as she put down her small bundle of firewood and built her cooking fire silently. As she cooked, she secretly planned her escape from the World-Above-the-World. She had grown tired of the Sun and longed for the evening and the night among her own people. "After all," she said to herself, "I only came into the sky to search for my child who had died, and I found him in little Anpao. So there is no reason for me to stay here or to fear the Sun. I have my own husband on earth and I have won over death both by entering the World-Above-the-World without dying and by reclaiming my child from the Sun. I am too clever to be caught!"

As soon as the Sun had left the tipi the next morning, the woman quickly gathered up her belongings and hurried to the hole in the sky. There she retied the rope to the root and then she tied the other end to her child Anpao.

"Do not cry," she whispered to the little boy, "you are made equally of earth and of sky, so nothing can happen to you. Do not whimper, Anpao; for soon we will be in our world where you will meet your own people!"

Then she carefully lowered Anpao through the hole in the sky, inch by inch, until the entire rope had been used. It stretched from the strong root in the World-Above-the-World through the hole in the sky—down, down, down ... *almost* to the earth below. The rope was not quite long enough.

"Oh!" cried the woman. "There is no time to make more rope! I will have to climb down and jump to the earth with little Anpao in my arms!"

And she quickly climbed through the hole and began her descent.

When she reached the end of the rope, she was very tired. With the last of her energy, she dangled off the end of the rope, but still she could not touch the earth. It was still far below her. She did not dare to untie Anpao, in order to make the rope longer, for fear of letting him fall. She was desperate and she cried out. But no one on earth heard her, and no one saw her and Anpao swinging helplessly in the wind.

"Oh!" the woman sighed. "I have wanted too much and now I have gotten nothing for all my efforts! Each time I have wanted too much and each time I have gotten nothing, but still I did not learn!"

The Sun came home to his tipi very tired that night and was surprised to find that his mistress and son were not there. He asked his old mother, but she had not seen them. He asked the stars, but they would not answer. So he went into the tipi and put some wood on the dying fire and waited for his family to come home. But still they did not return and it was now the darkest part of the night.

The Sun grew very weary but he could not sleep. He was worried about his son and his mistress. When the Moon came into the dark sky, she laughed at the Sun. "Ho ho, the Sun cannot see despite all his gold. He cannot see what is happening to him! Ho ho, go and look for your mistress from the World-Below. See what she has done to you, my foolish husband!" And the Moon laughed and went behind a cloud to mock the Sun, for she had recently discovered that he had a secret wife and child.

The Sun became angry and flames burst from his head as he ran from his tipi and searched the ground. By the Moon's bright light, the woman's trail was easy for the Sun to follow. "Foolish woman!" her husband barked. "She was in such a hurry to run away from me that she did not even brush over her tracks!"

At last the Sun came to the place where there was a hole in the sky. Instantly, he understood what had happened and looked down through the hole. He could see his small son, tied halfway down, and the wife hanging at the end of the rope, her moccasins just brushing the tips of the tallest trees of the earth. Now the Sun was very angry. He roared only once and then reached into the sky and plucked the branch of a willow and bent it into a hoop. At the touch of his hands, the hoop dried instantly and turned a deep red, for red is the color of the Sun. Then the Sun stood by the hole in the sky with the ring in his strong hands.

"Go, hoop," he ordered, "roll down the rope. Jump over the child and do not harm him. Roll down the rope, hoop! And when you reach the woman at the end, hit her on the head and kill her! This is what the Sun commands of you, and if you do it well, you and all your children will live in the shade beside the ponds and never feel the anger of the Sun. Go now, hoop, and do what I have ordered!"

The Sun spit on the hoop four times and, with a flash of his hand, he rolled it down the rope. The hoop flew into motion like a wheel of fire, spinning from the World-Above-the-World down the long rope the woman had made. The fiery hoop leaped over Anpao without touching him. But when it got to the mistress of the Sun, it burst into flame and made a noise like thunder. The woman opened her mouth and reached with her feet for the grass of the earth, but the wind swung her up into the air farther away from the ground. Then the hoop struck the woman, and her head fell back and her neck bent and she was dead.

When the root that held the rope in the World-Above-the-World felt the tug of the woman's dead body, it sagged with pity for her and the rope slipped away. The Sun roared fiercely and snatched for the rope as it whipped past him and through the hole in the sky. But he was not fast enough. The dead woman dropped to the earth. And the little boy, Anpao, fell too, plummeting down and landing on his mother so hard that her belly was split open, and where her blood stained his cheek a deep scar appeared.

When Anpao awakened from the terrible impact of the fall, he could not remember that he was the son of the Sun. All he could recall was that his name was Anpao. He looked around and found himself in a new world and he was afraid and began to cry. He could not see his father the Sun who stormed in anger and made the sky grow dark. He could only see his mother where she lay silent in the grass. Anpao was afraid to leave her side, and so he clung close to her and wept. But she did not move or speak, and soon it became very cold and dark as the grieving Sun slouched away in a great gloom. Anpao was alone and hungry and frightened.

Near the place where the mistress of the Sun had fallen to the earth, an old woman lived all by herself. She was very lonely and had no one to talk to and no one to hunt for her. But she was very wise. One day a stranger had given her a marvelous gourd. She had dried its seeds instead of eating them, and when the seeds were very dry, she carefully planted them in the ground near her house.

Since that day the old woman had a bright green garden topped with fruit. Every day at dawn, she would go from her tipi to the field to work among the vines and to sing sweetly to them so they would grow.

When the old woman was working in her field she always left her tipi flap open. Perhaps, she hoped, someone might come to visit her. And if her tipi were open, the person might not pass by but might rest inside until she came home at night. Then she could have a nice visit!

Anpao grew so hungry that he could stay with his dead mother no longer. He wandered away and found the old woman's tipi. He went inside, hoping to find something to eat and a fire at which to warm himself. But no sooner had Anpao entered the tipi than he became terrified. What if a horrible spirit lived here! He sobbed in fear and ran away, hiding beside his dead mother and cowering in the shadows of the tall grass.

But he had left his footprints on the floor of the tipi, and when the old woman came home at nightfall, she knew immediately that she had had a visitor. "But whose child could this be who came to my tipi?" she asked herself as she built a fire and began to cook dinner. "Oh, how fine it would be if the child came back and stayed to keep me company!"

The next morning Anpao awoke and was so tormented by hunger that he cautiously went back to the tipi of the old woman. But once again he was frightened and only stayed long enough to snatch the bit of food which the old woman had been wise enough to leave out for him. Then he ran back to his mother's side and tugged at her and offered her some of his food. But she would not respond. So he wept as he ate.

When the old lady returned to her tipi that night, she was delighted to see Anpao's fresh footprints. "Aha," she murmured happily. "Now how can I get this child and keep him here as my son?"

So each day the old woman left food where the child could reach it. When she came home at night the food was always gone, but there was no trace of the child except the little footprints all about the tipi. "Aha, he has escaped again. Now, let me see, how am I going to capture this marvelous child?" she wondered. Then she sat by her fire and listened to the owl and listened to the cricket. And eventually she thought out a plan.

Early the next day, the old woman lay down on the floor of her tipi close to the poles that made the sides. She lay silently until finally she heard someone coming.

She was a holy woman and understood many things. "Aha," she whispered. "Something not quite human is coming." She watched the door, and soon a very beautiful child with a curious scar on his face crept into her tipi. After seeing that no one moved inside, the boy quickly found the food the old woman had left for him. He sat on the floor, where he became so engrossed in eating that he did not notice when the old woman stood up in front of the door. But when she spoke to him, the child jumped to his feet in a terrible panic and tried to run past her. She prevented him from escaping, and when he hid under a fur robe, she tried to comfort him as he lay half-hidden.

"No, no, little sunshine-child, you cannot go to your mother anymore. I have found her body in the grass and she is dead. You have no mother, and you must not cry forever. I will be your grandmother. And we will live here and be happy."

To comfort Anpao further, she picked him up from his hiding place and carried him on her back the way his mother had carried him. Then she sat down on the floor, holding him snugly, and very soon the child stopped trembling and whimpering and fell asleep.

"This is no ordinary child." The old woman smiled knowingly. "I can feel his great power and I can see his future like the rings of an ancient tree."

The next morning the little boy awakened and smiled, for he saw the old woman huddled over the fire cooking something that smelled very good.

"Hello, little sunshine," she said and smiled when he crept next to her and peered hungrily into the fire. "You must call me Grandmother Spider, for I am the Spider Woman, the mother and comforter of all living beings and all things that grow. And you—who are you and who is your father?" But Anpao could not remember. "And what will we call you, little sunshine?"

At this the boy stood up proudly and said, "I am called Anpao!"

And so Anpao and Grandmother Spider lived very happily in the tipi near the green gourd field. In the golden light of Anpao's great father, Grandmother Spider made bowls of clay and baked them in the sunshine until they dried. Then she baked them again in the embers of her cooking fire. She gathered the thorny leaves of the yucca and coiled them into baskets. And then Anpao and Grandmother Spider went out into the autumn days to collect dried plants and to bring them home, where they were stored for the winter in the new baskets. Then they hung the yellow gourds to dry and they smoked meat over the fire.

When Anpao left the tipi in the morning, Grandmother Spider would say, "Look well, my child, at whatever you see." And in the evening, on his return for dinner, she would question him about every detail of what he had seen that day.

"Tell me, Anpao," Grandmother Spider would ask, "on which side of the tree is the lighter-colored bark? On which side do trees have the most regular branches?"

Every evening Grandmother Spider asked Anpao to name all the new birds he had seen during the day. He would name them according to their color or the shape of their bills or their songs or the location of their nests. Then Grandmother Spider would teach Anpao the correct names of the birds. If occasionally Anpao named a bird correctly by himself, Grandmother Spider would commend him warmly and make him feel very proud.

"Tell me," Grandmother Spider would ask at dinner, "how do you know if there are fish in a lake?"

"Because they would surely jump out of the water for flies at midday!"

Then she would smile patiently and explain. "What do you think, my child, makes the little pebbles group together under the shallow water? What makes the pretty curved marks in the sandy bottom and on the little sandbank? Where do you find the fish-eating birds? Have the inlets and outlets of the lake anything to do with my question, Anpao? Think on it, my child; think on it carefully. The world is full of signs and you must learn to read them."

If Anpao was lazy and did not make careful observations of the world around him, Grandmother Spider would sigh and say to him, "Anpao, my child, you must follow the example of the wolf. Even when he is surprised and runs for his very life, he will always pause to take one last careful look at you before he runs into his hiding place. So you too must take a second careful look at everything you see. All the animals are our teachers, but we must watch for the signs they give us if we are to learn anything about the world.

"For instance, you must never approach a grizzly bear's den from the front. You must steal up behind and then throw your blanket or a stone in front of his hole. He does not usually rush out for it; first he puts his head out and listens carefully, and then he comes out indifferently and sits on his great haunches on the mound in front of his cave before he makes any attack. While he is exposing himself in this way, my boy, you must aim at his heart. Always be as collected and calm as the animal himself. It is from the creatures that we can learn to be clever. These are the lessons of the world, and each day you can increase your wisdom if you will only look and keep all that you see."

One day when Grandmother Spider was preparing to go out to work, Anpao asked if he could stay home. "Don't you want to go with me into the field and sing to the plants?" the old woman asked.

"No, Grandmother Spider," he said, "I would rather stay here today and play with my hoop."

"Very well, you may stay home, because you are a good boy and always work very hard. But you must be careful not to throw your hoop into the air, or something bad could happen to you. Mind what your old Grandmother Spider has told you, for she knows many things. You may roll the hoop on the earth but you must not throw it into the air. Do you understand?"

"Yes, Grandmother," answered Anpao, but naturally he wondered what could happen to him if he threw his hoop high into the air. "Ah," he thought, "nothing bad will happen to *me!*"

So when Grandmother Spider had left, he took his hoop and went outside into the sunshine. He played with the hoop for a short time—then he could no longer resist the temptation to toss it into the air to see what might happen. Before the Sun could warn him, Anpao tossed the hoop. Up and up it went, as high as the world from which Anpao had fallen. Then, very gracefully and slowly, the hoop began to fall from the sky. As it fell, it moved faster and still faster until it landed right on Anpao's head with a terrible crash. For a moment the child stood in amazement. The hoop went right down through his entire body and cut him in two!

"Oh!"

"Oh!"

That is what two voices said at exactly the same time. There was no longer one child standing there, but two. They were identical except that one was right-handed and the other was left-handed.

"Well," said the twin to Anpao, "that is amazing! And tell me, who are you?"

"Me?" said Anpao. "That is obvious! I am I! But who are you?"

"Me?" said the twin. "That is very obvious! I too am I!"

And the two half-boys looked at each other in amazement for a long time. Finally Anpao understood. "Ah," he said, "I am I and you are I—but when we are together, we are we."

"And we are stronger as we than each of us is by himself," said the twin. "Is that true, brother-twin?"

"Yes, that must be true. That means we can hurl our hoop very high! Come, let's play!"

So Anpao, who was now twins, began to play.

When the sunlight faded and the shadows of the trees stretched across the rich black soil, the twins saw Grandmother Spider coming home from the field.

"Oh our goodness," said the twins. "We think Grandmother will be very angry when she finds that there are two of us!"

The old woman came closer and kept peering at the two boys, who hugged each other and cowered in fear of Grandmother Spider's anger. "Anpao! What have you done and who is that with you there in the dim light?" she shouted as she came closer.

"We are here," the twins answered together.

"Ah," the old woman sighed, "something is wrong with my poor eyes. I see two of you."

"Please, Grandmother Spider, don't be too angry with us. There is nothing wrong with your eyes," the twins said together; "we who were once one are now two."

"Aha," sighed Grandmother Spider. "Now I understand what has happened. It is a great pity, for now our happy times must end. When you were young, you were one with my house. But now you have become your own friend. Now there is nothing I can do to keep you here. You must go off, my dear sunshine-children, and find your adventures among the places beyond the world."

"But, Grandmother Spider, we were so happy here with you! Please, don't make us go away!" the twins begged.

"My children, it is done and cannot be undone. That is the way it always is. We are free to do what we wish; but we must also accept whatever comes of it. That is the way it is. So, my children, you can stay until the morning. But then you must go out of my tipi forever and find the path that is your own. Great trials are in your future and you must be prepared for them. In distant places, where even the eagle does not fly, there is great trouble. Unless you are prepared, it will, like an avalanche, tumble over you and over all our people, and we shall be destroyed."

"But where will we find these enemies?" the twins asked.

"You will recognize them when you come to the place where they are," Grandmother Spider told them. "Do not be deceived by them. They will tell you that they are good and that they wish you well. They will promise you many things that you know are impossible. Slowly, as you listen to them, you will come to hope for what cannot be. The Evil Ones will tell you that you must be something which you cannot be and ridicule you when you fail to become what you cannot become. That is why they are evil. They are unreal and no one can fight them. We poor people cannot see through them," Grandmother Spider told the twins in a whisper, as if the Evil Ones hovered over her as she spoke. "Now," she said more loudly, glancing to her left, "come, my children, let us eat together for the last time and then you must sleep and be ready for your journey."

They sat on the floor of the tipi and ate together in the light of the fire. And in the morning when the fire had grown small, the half-boys went out into the daylight and found a pathway that led to distant places where the eagles do not fly. They looked back to wave to Grandmother Spider. She stood alone by her tipi and wept as she watched her boys leave.

"Be brave!" she shouted to the half-boys. "Bring us great honor!" Then she shouted again, "Be brave and kind. Open yourselves to strangers and do not fear what you do not know. Good-by, my children. Do not forget your Grandmother Spider!"

All That Happened Must Happen Again

Again the sacred pipe was lighted, and under the new day it was passed around the great circle where the twins slept and the old swan-woman rose as a small flame among the coals of the dying fire.

"Ah," she said, and laughed. "Foolish boys, you who seek the Sun and wish to beg a wife from him.... Ha, foolish boys, you yourselves are sons of the Sun! But no! Do not awaken them yet! Let them sleep. Sleep, sons of the Sun, for the dream is not over. You have to swim a vast river of dreams before you may finally awaken. Before you find the beautiful Ko-ko-mik-e-is and her sad little village, you must begin your long journey from the tipi of Grandmother Spider and travel over great prairies, through perilous canyons in which the water leaps, along wooded ridges, and among the grassy valleys. You must watch the trees loosen their leaves and you must see the snow tumble over the silent winter's ground. All that you have done you must do again. You must grow from boys into young men, as you search the sky for the Sun. You must become men among men, as you are chased by the Moon and your robes become ugly and your sack of food grows smaller and you are afraid you will starve. Do you see? Your poor robes have become poorer and the wind hisses its disregard for your trembling. And just when you are about to give up your quest, you suddenly discover the village where Ko-ko-mik-e-is lives. And then, do you recall? Yes, you fall in love. Do you recall the day you fell in love, foolish boys? And do you recall that you were sent to find the great Sun? And after a long search you found an old striped-face woman...yes, you found her and she fed you. And then what did you do? Ha! foolish boys, you went up to the top of the Hill-Above-the-Sky and you insulted the Moon! Yes, you did! I heard you say that the Moon is the ugliest thing you have ever seen! So do not deny it! That is why the darkness came and that is why you cried out in fear!"

"Help!" shouts Anpao, reaching to embrace his sleeping brother. But no one is lying beside him now. He jumps to his feet and shouts again and again, but still there is no reply. A terrible feeling sweeps over Anpao. He trembles and can barely stand up.

"Ah-ha," cackles the old woman, shaking her tattered robe and leaping high into the air again and again, higher and higher.

"Look!" the old woman hisses, crawling to his feet and pointing into the sky, as Anpao slowly turns in dread and sees a black leafless tree with something...something...hanging from its branches.

"Go ahead, foolish boy," she whines into his ear. "Go ahead and take a closer look." But Anpao is unable to move.

"Go ahead," she repeats again and again. "Go-ahead, go-ahead, go-ahead-go-ahead."

Unwillingly, he creeps toward the tree, as the sweat runs down his neck and a terrible sickness grips his stomach. As he climbs toward the summit of the shadowy hill, the air around him catches on fire and everything glistens with a frigid light. The little campfire suddenly explodes into a million blue sparks, which cling like mosquitoes to the soft pelt of the black sky. Anpao covers his head and staggers upward. And as he approaches a thing that is hanging from the tree, he tries with all his power to awaken from his dream, but he cannot. As he comes closer to the terrible thing dangling from the tree, he cannot resist reaching out for it ... touching it with trembling fingers. It is cold. And it is soft ... and wet. It is hanging by its feet, the hair-entangled head swinging ever so gently in a freezing breeze.

"Go ahead," the old woman sings softly in his ear. "Go ahead ... go ahead ... go ahead."

Anpao fearfully draws the thing toward him to see if it has a face. "Ah!" he screams as the lightning bursts. "Ah!" he bellows, pulling back from the horrible, dead, white face.

"Bastard-child!" the face shrieks at him. "Little bastard of my faithless husband!" it screams, as Anpao falls back and stares into the gleaming white eyes of the Moon. "You squealing little bastard-child! Did you think you could fool the Moon? You half-thing! Did you think I would help you get your wretched little Ko-ko-mik-e-is?" And she twists her mouth and howls, thrusting out with her claws and ripping across Anpao's face.

"Ah!" he screams with pain, as the blood pours over his cheeks and blinds him. "Ah!" he wails, backing away deliriously and trying to wipe the blood from his eyes.

But the Moon leaps from the black tree and leers at him with her terrible, vacant eyes as she throws down the disguise of the old swan-woman. Suddenly her long white wings explode into crystals of frozen light. "Bastard-boy! You are dying! Can't you feel the death inside your body, hatching from a million tiny eggs! You are going where your wretched mother has gone!"

"Oh, no!" howls Anpao, as he falls back and stumbles with a groan, grappling blindly, clutching the fierce wound on his face, and staggering to his feet as the Moon tosses her blazing crystals at him. "Ah!" he cries desperately, as he hurtles down the steep hill, yelling frantically and plunging away from that terrible sight . . . falling . . . falling again and again against the stinging trees as he plunges into the forest of nettles . . . collapsing at the edge of the bubbling yellow river . . . calling out for his lost brother. Then the night turns orange and scarlet and purple . . . and black.

"*Kyi!*" Anpao groaned when he awoke. He could see two little eyes very close to him. He sat up in horror. Suddenly a great flock of yellow birds leaped into the air with a rush of wings. A fierce wind blew over him. Then it was quiet.

The fire was cold. The camp was entirely deserted. Anpao found himself alone. The old woman was gone. The sky was a hazy void without Moon or Sun. Everything was gone. Only Oapna remained, curled up and motionless beside the dead fire.

But Oapna had changed into some unimaginable thing. It was astonishing. Anpao lay helplessly on the ground, for roots had grown over his body while he had lain unconscious. In the silence he stared at his brother, who had changed into something he had never seen before. He had turned golden and fibrous and hard—like a gigantic cocoon. He had become a blank, membranous gourd, inside of which Anpao could see Oapna's translucent body slowly pulsating.

Then gradually five wet fingers burst one at a time through the thin wall of the cocoon, and the body began breaking out bit by bit, until at last a moist, glistening new Oapna lay in the cradle of the sodden membrane. This newly born body feebly rubbed its limbs together to dry itself and undulated blindly like a great worm. Then after it had rested, it began to slide toward Anpao.

"Ah," Anpao whimpered, as he lay frozen, feeling the rubbery limbs slowly overtake him. "Ah," he murmured, as he tried to break free, dazed with fear as this cocoon-brother rolled upon him and gradually dissolved, finger by finger, leg by leg, eye by eye, into Anpao's body. "Ah," he sobbed. And finally Oapna vanished utterly, and where there had been two boys there was now only one.

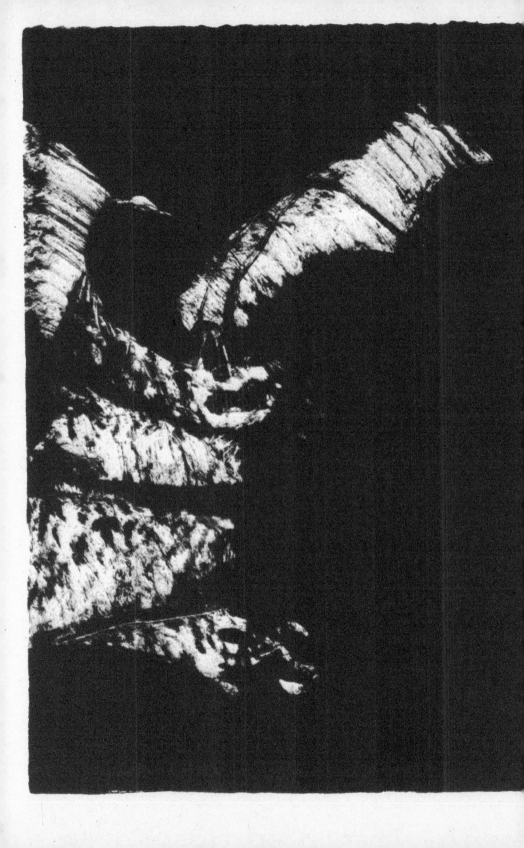

III

The Lessons of Heaven and Earth

The Sky Beings

In the distance Anpao could see the Sun. It shone brighter
than ever before, warming him and giving him courage.
He turned his back on the encampment of the Moon. "I
am not afraid of the Moon," he exclaimed to his father, the
Sun. "Because terror and torment are as imperfect as courage
and contentment. My Grandmother Spider tried to teach me
that lesson, but I was too young to understand. She would
be pleased that I have found a vision from the dark side of
the Moon. Now I can see light through the imperfections of
the darkness. And I have become a person with a memory of
the past and with a vision of the future.

"It is like an apple," Anpao declared happily. "How
can such an amazing fruit come into existence? How can
each apple know that it must become an apple? Yes, my
father, an apple is a very difficult thing, but for the apple
tree it is easy."

The colorless camp where the Moon had tricked him
was left behind, and Anpao began to sing to himself as he
climbed the steep, rugged trail into the mountains.

"Where the mountain crosses
on top of the mountain, I do not know where it is.

I wander where my spirit and my heart are lost,
but my feet know the way
. . . this is my dream song.
Ah, my friends, please hear me."

He traveled among the great boulders all that day and all that night, singing his dream song. He thought of Grandmother Spider, and her teachings stayed with him and so did the power of her wisdom. When he camped and made a fire and hunted for food, all that Grandmother Spider had taught him helped him to survive. When he awoke and rolled his possessions into skin sacks, her lessons showed him how to make his burden easy. And when he searched for a good path, Grandmother Spider's teachings helped him find his way.

On the fifth day of his long journey from the camp of the Moon, Anpao came to a place that he had never seen before. It was filled with great streams, waterfalls, and valleys of stinging nettles. The narrow trail became narrower and narrower, until at last it came to an end at the brink of a deep chasm. In order to continue along his way, Anpao had to cross the ravine on a fallen tree which was soggy with moss and glistened with the spray of the waterfall. As he carefully picked his way over the slippery tree-bridge, someone suddenly called out to him. Anpao spun around and caught a glimpse of a boy peering at him from behind a tree. But before he could speak to the stranger, he lost his footing and fell backward into empty space.

"Oh!" he cried out in pain, for his leg was twisted under him, and when he tried to get up he could tell that it was broken. "Ah," he exclaimed. "Someone please help me! You up there, can you hear me? Please, do not leave me here without help!"

The boy came out from behind the tree and crept quickly over the bridge without looking down, acting as if he could not hear Anpao's call for help. For just a moment he hesitated and Anpao's hope rose. Then the boy hurried away.

The pain in his leg was becoming so terrible that Anpao felt dizzy. Gradually the stones beneath him turned into feathers and he could hear the rushing of water. Then the night surrounded him and he could hear nothing.

When he opened his eyes he found himself at the bottom of the deep crevasse into which he had fallen. His leg was badly swollen and ached so horribly that he could barely clutch at consciousness. He could not sit up, and yet he could not stay pinned to the jagged rocks and sharp branches and bushes on which he had fallen. When he summoned a great effort and managed to turn around, he discovered a stout stick which he thought he might use as a crutch. But the pain pierced his back and leg, and no amount of effort and endurance could get him to his feet. Surely he would die if someone did not happen along to find him.

And that was when he saw the little man who seemed to have been sitting very close by all the time. He was extremely old and ugly, his skin was gray and pitted, and his scalp lock had grown very long and straggly. He sat silently, blinking his little eyes and staring blankly at Anpao. Behind him, in the side of the ravine, was a cave which Anpao had not noticed.

For a long time they simply looked at each other. It seemed that the old man had absolutely no intention of doing anything but stare at Anpao. Perhaps he was lingering, rather than sneaking away like that wretched boy, in the hope that Anpao would die before his eyes.

"Hello," Anpao said desperately, hoping the fellow would not run away at the first sound of his voice. He did not, but neither did he do anything else. He simply continued to stare blankly at Anpao.

"What are you called?" Anpao asked.

"I am called," the old man said mockingly, "the Man-Who-Lives-Here!" And he laughed rather nastily.

"Please pity me and help me," Anpao urged, as the pain grew worse and he feared he would faint once again. But the old man said nothing. He sat on a rock as gray as he was and peered intently at Anpao's face and leg and at his sack of possessions, which had also plummeted into the ravine.

"Are you a fool or a wise man?" the man asked vacantly. "No, do not tell me!" he snapped. "You'll ruin the fun! Let me guess!" Again he laughed as he got up on his short little legs and stared aimlessly into Anpao's pain-wracked face. "Ah, let me see, let me see. You must be a fool because you have broken your leg and you are about to starve to death down here in this ravine!"

"Please, old man, do not make fun of me. I cannot move. Please, you must help me!"

"Help yourself," the ugly old man cackled, as he turned to leave.

"No! Please don't go away! Please stay here for just a little while longer!"

"Why? Are you going to do something interesting?" the old man asked. "Of course, if you are going to dance or make funny gestures, then certainly I wouldn't want to miss it because we have very little fun in this forest. But if all you plan to do is lie there and weep and die, I don't want to stay because I have already seen many people do that." And again he turned to leave.

"Oh, please! Whoever you are, I am sorry if I have offended you! I don't know why you are angry with me! And I apologize if I have said or done something I should not have done! But please don't go away and leave me here! You must help me!"

At this the old man laughed so hard he had to sit down. "I have heard many things from fools," he cried, as he roared with merriment, "but never have I been told that I must help a fool to live! That is so amusing that perhaps I should do something for you. Tell me, are you always so funny, or is it just when you have fallen into a ravine and broken your nasty little leg? No! Don't tell me, let me guess. Ah, let me see, perhaps you can give me a little hint. Go ahead, give me just a little hint. But not a big one! Just a little hint!"

But Anpao could not speak. He threw back his head in agony and tried desperately to remain conscious, for he knew that, if he passed out and the old man left him, he could not survive alone.

"Ah, you are tired," the man cooed. "Well, then, perhaps you should stay here with me and do exactly what I tell you and perhaps you won't die after all." The old man smiled nastily as he walked slowly around Anpao and inspected him carefully.

"Perhaps if you obey me, you will be all right after all," he said, and squatted next to Anpao and sniffed at him several times. Then he took him by the hair and pulled his head back and looked into Anpao's half-closed eyes. "Is there anybody in there?" he said, and giggled.

Anpao panted and tried to nod his head to the man. He gasped for breath and swallowed again and again, trying to moisten his parched mouth so he could speak. "Thank you, thank you," he groaned. But the old man said nothing. He sat beside Anpao with an aimless smile on his face, and his eyes rolled in his head.

When Anpao had gathered enough strength to speak, he smiled weakly and asked again, "Please, what are you called?"

"I am called the Man-Who-Just-Sniffed-You!" He gave Anpao a look of disapproval. "You smell bad. You smell very bad. But I need someone to hunt for me. I am too old to do anything but eat and sleep and fart. But I am clever. I am very clever. And I can cure you. Yes, that is what I said, I can cure you if you promise to stay here with me and bring me whatever food you find."

Anpao was silent. He needed the old man's help, but he did not want to stay with him. He wanted to run away. He wanted to escape and continue his search for the Sun.

"Are you listening, fool? I said to you: I will save your

worthless life," the man shouted, staring intently at Anpao, "but you must promise to take care of me in return!"

"All right . . . all right!"

"Promise!"

"Yes, I promise. I promise."

The old man laughed delightedly and hopped onto his little legs and scurried away. When he returned he brought water in a gourd, and in another gourd dried leaves like none Anpao had ever seen. He winked incessantly and moved his purple tongue over his lips as he soaked the herbs in the water. Then he spread the compress over the wound on Anpao's leg and bound it with strips of soft hide. "Now, Goat-Person, you will be healed," he said, and giggled. "Perhaps you think that only holy people can cure, but it is not true. Like most of what you think, it is not true, Goat-Person."

"My name is not Goat-Person."

"Yes, I know that," snapped the little man. "It is Anpao, and you have an ugly scar on your face, and though I have saved your life you are already acting as if you are somebody important—and you are only a goat or a potato or dried dung! But I need a strong young man to hunt for me, so I can't be too choosy." Then he laughed evilly and spit on Anpao's leg.

In a few days Anpao felt well again and, though he hated the old man, he went out to hunt food for him in order to honor his promise. Sometimes he tracked a deer which permitted itself to be killed so Anpao and the old man would have meat to eat. At times the meat was so heavy that Anpao could not carry it back to the cave by himself, so the old man would grumble and creep from his shelter to help bring the kill back to the camp.

The old man would not allow Anpao to sleep inside the cave. "Poo, you smell bad!" he grunted nastily. Even when the winter cold came, Anpao had to find shelter in the ravine. All that winter he hunted for the old man and took care of him as he had promised. He withstood all his cruel comments and vicious criticism. But he stayed away as much as he could, for the ugly old fellow liked to hit him with a stick or poke him with a spear, cackling insanely all the while.

Anpao never attempted to escape by climbing the walls of the ravine. He obeyed the old man and never ventured beyond the rocky canyon surrounding the cave. When at last the winter was over and warm winds came down the slopes and animals that had slept all winter long came out of their dens, Anpao knew it was spring and he would lie awake and stare into the starry night dreaming of Ko-ko-mik-e-is.

One day he found the tracks of a great bear and followed them, climbing high on the canyon walls, across the narrow ridges, and to the edge of a deep forest. Suddenly there was a great roar and the bear came into view. It was black and stood very tall and, when it saw Anpao, it opened its arms wide. In an instant Anpao lifted his bow, and his arrow struck the bear in the heart. It fell with a great crash and Anpao cautiously approached the huge carcass. Just at the moment when he bent over the bear, Anpao heard strange voices behind him. He whirled around in fear and raised his bow. Four men stood in a mist. They were dressed unlike any people he had ever seen—in strange robes of cloud. "Please tell me, who are you and what do you want here?" Anpao asked them, trying not to be afraid.

In response there came a resounding rumble in the sky. "We are Thunder," the cloud-men intoned together. "But we are not your enemies. We are looking for a little old man who lives hidden in a ravine in these mountains. He is evil and we want to find him."

"I know the man you are seeking," Anpao said. "He is indeed evil, but he saved my life and so I do as he tells me and I hunt for him. Surely he is the one you are seeking, because he is the only person who lives in these mountains. I have been here a long time and you are the first people I have ever seen besides the old man."

"Are you happy with this life he makes you live?" the Thunders asked.

"No, I am not. I want to leave this place, but I gave my promise to stay."

"If you are willing to help us find the old man, we will set you free to go wherever you wish."

Anpao studied the strangers with uncertainty. Perhaps they too wanted to make him work for them and would not let him go after he had showed them where the old man lived. But there was something about the faces and eyes of these strangers that reassured Anpao, and so he said, "Yes, I will help you."

"Then do exactly as we tell you. First, go to the old man and tell him you have killed this great black bear and need his help to carry the meat home. He loves bear fat and so he will come here and help you. But be careful of him, for he is very sly. You may have to coax him to venture so far from his home and so close to the forest, but do whatever you must to bring him here. Do you understand?"

Anpao gazed doubtfully at the Thunders. "Yes," he said. "I understand." And he decided that he would do what these cloud-people asked of him.

When Anpao arrived at the cave, the old man shouted at him and scolded him for leaving the ravine. But his scowl turned into a greedy grin when he learned of Anpao's sumptuous kill. "Ha ha!" he snickered as he ran into the cave and hastily sharpened his stone knife, muttering to himself about the fat meat he would have for dinner. When he was ready, he called Anpao and they started off—the old man scurrying ahead in his eagerness to see the bear.

"Ahuh, I see it!" the old man cackled happily as they came upon the great carcass of the bear. "Oh, my, it is very large indeed! You are a good hunter to have killed so great a bear!"

And at once the old man started to work skinning and cutting the carcass as fast as he could. Anpao stood in silence, watching the ugly old man as he worked nervously, stopping often to glance around him.

"Hurry, hurry, and get to work," he muttered urgently, as he cut the animal into pieces. "Why are you just standing there! Get to work, Goat-Person, or I will send you away

into the forest where you will stumble and kill yourself!"
As he said this, he never took his eyes off the forest around
him and the sky above. Anpao could see that the old man
was afraid of being so far from his ravine and from the
cave.

"Hurry!" the old man barked. "Hurry up and put the
meat on my back! More! More!" he ordered. "Do as I tell
you. Pile it on my shoulders quickly!"

Anpao worked as fast as he could, amazed at how
much weight the old man could carry. By now it was getting
quite dark and the old man seemed more and more anxious.

"Ah," the old man whispered. "It could rain.... Yes, I
think it could. Tell me, do you think it will rain? Do you see
any clouds moving in this direction?"

"No, the sky is perfectly clear," Anpao told him, as
they started home, the old man bent over under his burden.

"Ah," groaned the old man. "Tell me if you see a cloud
—even a very little cloud! Tell me if you see anything that
even looks like a cloud! Do you understand?"

"Yes," Anpao assured him with a grin.

Soon a cloud appeared in the distance. Anpao watched
silently as it glided across the sky. As the cloud came closer
it also grew larger, until it lingered just above them and
gradually turned dark and angry. The last light of day
quickly fell back under the black cloud, which by now
was so vast that it covered the entire sky above them. When
the old man saw his shadow suddenly vanish from the ground
in front of him, he cried out and allowed the great load
of meat to fall to the ground. Just at that moment the

Thunders stepped from the folds of the cloud and confronted the terrified old man.

"So we have found you at last!" they shouted at him. But before their billowing robes could envelop him, the old man leaped out of their reach and started running as fast as his little bowed legs would carry him.

Anpao was astonished to see the old man leap over the ground, running so quickly that he was almost invisible. But the Thunders raised a fearful roar and the wind came and great boulders crashed to the ground all around their enemy. These rocks formed a wall which trapped the old man, who, finding himself cornered, hissed and spit and slashed the air with his hands. But the Thunders laughed loudly, and rocks began to tumble down upon the old man. For a moment he sprang up and, arching his back like a giant porcupine, began shooting poisoned quills at his enemies. But the Thunders turned the quills aside and laughed again so loudly that the earth shook.

The old man scrambled over the boulders to make an escape. The night burst with lightning as the Thunders spit into their palms and threw sizzling bolts at the fleeing old man. Just as he reached his cave, the air exploded with blue sparks and lightning struck him. For a moment his body glowed like a torch, and great flames leaped from the top of his head. Then he fell slowly to the ground, where his body smoldered until at last it vanished entirely.

"We have finished our task with your help," the Thunders told Anpao, as they looked at the gray ashes of the evil old one. "He was a very wicked power," they said. "He made slaves of young people and worked them to death. He pretended to be an old man so no one would expect him to do any work. It is good that he is gone. Now, Anpao, you are free of him."

"I thank you," Anpao told the cloud-people. "I wish to honor you for what you have done."

"Perhaps one day we will come back for you, Anpao, and ask for your help. But now you are tired and you are hungry. If you will put on this robe of clouds, we will take you to a village nearby. There you will find friends. Come."

They gave Anpao a glistening cloud-robe and showed him how to move the wings which they had carefully fastened to his shoulders with soft hide. Then with a marvelous gust of wind they were suddenly aloft among the swirling leaves, sailing through the night so high that Anpao could faintly hear the songs of the stars.

When Anpao reached the village, the people were sitting around their fire. They shouted with pleasure when they saw the cloud-people swoop down over their lodges, and they welcomed Anpao to their fireside. After eating a good meal, Anpao thanked his new friends by telling them the story of the Thunders, and how they had freed him from the evil one who had enslaved him in the ravine.

As Anpao recounted his story, he caught sight of a familiar face just beyond the fire's light. It was the boy who had ignored Anpao's call for help and left him in the ravine to die. Anpao took pity on the boy and did not tell the people of his village how badly he had treated a stranger. All night the boy feared that he would be exposed, and so he hid from Anpao. But Anpao wanted no vengeance. Besides, his stories had won him the admiration of all the men of the village, and his popularity made the offending boy all the more miserable about his behavior. After talking late into the night with the young men and answering their many questions about his adventures, Anpao was so tired that he wanted nothing more of his hosts than a safe place to sleep. He had worked hard and eaten little during the long months of his imprisonment, and when at last he was given a place to sleep, he curled up by the warm fire under a beautiful fur and smiled blissfully as he began to snore.

The next day, one of the proudest young men of the village and his younger brother approached Anpao and humbly asked him to be their friend. Anpao was delighted, for he had been without the comradeship of men his own age for a long time. The three friends made arrows and went hunting together. As the weeks passed, and they taught one another songs and told one another secrets, the three became inseparable, and all the people of the village hoped that perhaps Anpao might settle down and live with them.

One night, after the three comrades had sung many songs, Anpao told them about Ko-ko-mik-e-is and of his quest for the Sun. He told them about the way he had been born and of his descent from the sky where his father lived. He told them about the death of his mother and about Grandmother Spider. He explained to his friends how he had become two and then become one again, and how he had come to possess a vision through a fearful lesson from the Moon.

"I would like to stay with your people and live here with you, but I do not belong here," Anpao told his two friends. "I must find the Sun and ask him to remove this scar from my face as a sign to Ko-ko-mik-e-is that she is free to marry me."

Though the brothers urged Anpao to forget about Ko-ko-mik-e-is and his search, Anpao would not listen to them. "We have girls here who are more beautiful than Ko-ko-mik-e-is!" they would boast. "Already there are very many girls who would like to be with you."

"No, my friends, I cannot stay with you. Once I am strong, I must continue my quest for the Sun. It is what I have been dreaming about and if I give up that dream I will become a sullen old fellow. No, my friends, I have grown to understand that it is not our enemies, but our friends and lovers, who keep us from our destinies. I must escape from them if I am to live."

Snake Boy

◆

When it was spring, and in the night the men of the clans could be heard singing to the spirits of powerful animals, Anpao and his two friends decided they would explore the lands beyond the village. The brothers had never ventured out of the valley of their people, for the elders often cautioned them about the dangers of the world beyond the meadow. But Anpao loved to explore, and his infatuation with adventure was highly contagious. Before long his two friends wanted to accompany him.

So early one morning the three young men started in the direction of the farthest slope of the little valley. By the time the Sun was high, they were tired and hungry. The brothers complained of the heat and cursed the rocks which bruised their feet through the thin soles of their moccasins. They were not the kind of people who are made for adventure.

Anpao attempted to encourage them, but his high spirits had little effect. The elder brother was especially sullen as they hiked through the rocky, scorched landscape in which nothing grew and there was neither fruit to eat nor water to drink. The three young men searched everywhere for food, but they found absolutely nothing, not even tender roots or green berries. Finally, the sullen elder brother sat down on a rock and refused to go any farther. "I want to turn back," he said angrily.

"No," protested the younger brother. "We have come this far and what will be the good of it if we turn back before we have seen what lies beyond the valley?"

"It takes nothing to go back," Anpao told them. "That is why people never get anywhere. Do not be so easily disappointed, my friend. We will find food soon. And we will also find a good place to make our camp for the night."

The elder brother grumbled but finally agreed to continue their journey. And so, after resting in the shade of a boulder, they started out again.

"Ah!" shouted the elder brother suddenly. "Just as you said, Anpao, I have found food! Come and see what I have found for us!"

The three young men crowded around a nest built of pebbles among the great rocks. In the nest were four extremely large greenish eggs. "I am very glad," the elder brother said, and laughed. "I have found a blessing. Here is food for us to eat in this place where there is no food!"

"No," Anpao whispered. "Please, my friends, do not eat these eggs. I think there is great power in them. We must come away and continue walking."

"You are a fool, Anpao," the elder brother shouted. "You always tell us what to do. If we are tired, you tell us we must continue to walk. If we are hungry, you tell us we must be patient. And when we finally find food, then you tell us we must not eat it. You are a fool and I don't know why I call you my friend!"

"Listen to me..." Anpao urged, but the brothers ignored him and gathered dried grass to make a fire. Soon the eggs were roasting. The brothers sang heartily, their voices echoing among the great gray rocks, as they sniffed the cooking food.

"You must listen to what I am telling you," Anpao pleaded. "I have come to know about such things, and you are doing evil. Already the eggs have died in the fire. Now we must run away quickly. You cannot steal these eggs without a prayer or an offering. A living thing is a vast mystery, and something which is coming into life, like these great eggs, is even more mysterious. I know that something bad will happen if we eat these eggs."

The younger brother looked worriedly at Anpao, and at last he agreed to abandon the eggs. But the elder brother laughed at both of them, as he carefully removed one of the eggs from the fire and broke it open. "Hmm," he sighed, "how good this egg is! Come, see how good they taste. Eat one before you die of hunger!" he mumbled as he ate greedily. But the other two refused to touch the eggs, so the hungry brother ate the two eggs he had cooked for his brother and Anpao as well as his own. After he had finished, he lay down and rested, while his brother and Anpao watched him with great apprehension. He mocked their concern and laughed at them, patting his belly proudly. "You are both starving fools! I am full and you are hungry. Come now, let us continue our journey while there is still light."

After they had walked for a considerable distance and nothing had happened, the younger brother began to regret that he had listened to Anpao's warning. He was so hungry he could think of nothing but how large and delicious-looking the eggs had been. He was about to chide Anpao for his advice when his brother suddenly complained of sharp pains in his stomach. He gradually turned horribly pale and was unwilling to walk.

But there was no place to stop, and nowhere for the sick brother to lie down and rest. Everywhere were sharp stones and the blaze of the Sun. So the young men continued across the white haze of the plain until at last the fierce sunlight withdrew and the world became cool and dark. They finally found a tiny ravine and searched for water. All they found was a muddy little stream flowing sluggishly through the clay and stones. There, among the thorny bushes and dry grass, the three young men made camp.

Just before daybreak, the elder brother awakened Anpao.

"Please help me," he whispered. "I am going to die. I cannot walk. My legs feel strange. I think something horrible is happening to me! Please," he begged in a strange voice, "you must help me, Anpao!"

"You must relax, my friend," Anpao told him softly. "Come, lie still and let me see what is wrong. Maybe there is something wrong with your legs from our long walk. Perhaps I can help you." So he drew back his friend's robe and took off his moccasins. It was true: something very peculiar was happening. The boy's legs were no longer smooth and brown. His skin had changed . . . not completely, but enough to make it a very curious sight. It had become scaly and seemed to have very faint green stripes.

"What is it, Anpao?" the boy asked in dread. But Anpao could not tell him. "What do you see, Anpao? Are my legs all right?"

"Yes, yes, I think they are fine," Anpao said softly.

"Ah," he sighed. "Then awaken my brother and let's go now. I am so thirsty I can't stand it. The water in the stream has dried up during the night and we have nothing to drink."

Anpao peered at the boy, for the stream was not dry but exactly as it had been when they found it.

"Quickly, quickly, let's go find water," the sick boy said in a daze. "I know I will feel fine if only we can find some water to drink!" Before Anpao could stop him, he had struggled to his feet and started out without waiting for the others. "We must go," he mumbled again and again, "we must go."

Anpao and the younger brother followed as quickly as they could. The elder brother moved quickly across the sharp, stony terrain, and his brother and Anpao could barely keep up with him. Finally, the boy stopped and looked as if he might collapse.

"Ah, help me!" he cried out. He was feeling worse and could walk no farther. His legs, he told them, were so heavy that they did not seem to be part of his body. They dragged behind him and would not do what he told them to do. Yet he insisted upon continuing, for he said that only water could cure him. So after resting a moment, he hurried on alone. Afraid to argue with him, his brother and Anpao ran after him and tried to support his body with their arms. Slowly the three friends staggered through the rocks and boulders.

"Please," the boy whimpered, "don't leave me—no matter what happens. I know I have been cruel to people. But I will surely die if you leave me here alone."

"We won't leave you," Anpao promised. "Try to walk and don't worry so much. We will stay with you until we find water and you are safe. We both promise this to you."

All that hot day they traveled painfully over the cruel landscape, exhausted from the heat and recoiling from the sharp stones which cut through their moccasins and bruised their feet.

Finally at nightfall they came to the edge of the terrible valley of rocks and found themselves in a beautiful wooded area where a small lake was fed by clear water cascading from the summit of the vast cliff that bordered the valley of rocks.

"Please," pleaded the sick boy, "let's make camp here. I want to be near the water. Perhaps if I sit with my legs in the cool water they will be cured. I am certain that if my legs are in the water they will get better." So his brother and Anpao carefully lowered him to the bank of the lake, where he sat and dangled his legs in the cold clear water.

"I will make a fire,"Anpao said. "Will you be all right without us? Your brother can look for food while I make the fire, if you can get along for a while." The sick boy assured them that he would be fine now that he was near the water. So they left him and went off to make camp and to find food.

As soon as they were gone, the boy quickly untied his hair ornaments and took off his breechclout and put them with his moccasins on the shore. Then he slipped quietly into the deep water and began to swim in the pale light of the rising Moon. He glided effortlessly through the water, diving gracefully and emerging again, twisting his body as he slithered through the water, and his skin gleamed in the moonlight.

"I feel marvelous!" he shouted to his brother and Anpao. "Now I feel better than I ever have felt in my life! Come and see how well I have learned to swim!"

"No," his young brother called desperately, rushing to the shore and searching the night for him. "Come out of the water! Please come out!"

Anpao had just lighted the campfire when he heard the sick boy calling from somewhere out in the middle of the lake. He too ran to the shore and called out, "Please, come back now and join us at the fire. It is warm and you can dry off."

"Yes, yes, yes," the boy said, laughing, as he dragged himself from the water, flopping down exhausted on the shore and panting for breath. "Ah!" he cried, looking down at his legs for the first time.

His legs had grown together, and the entire lower part of his body was now covered with green scales. "What is happening to me!" he bellowed in panic.

His brother tried to comfort him, and together he and Anpao managed to carry him to the fireside, where they begged him to rest. They did not let the sick boy realize how frightened they were, but when he finally closed his eyes they looked at each other in astonishment and the younger brother sobbed quietly. In the light of the fire they could see stripes gradually covering the body of the sleeping boy.

That night the younger brother and Anpao could not rest. The sick brother whimpered continually, and once he awakened in hysterics and begged them to cast him into the lake and forget him. It was a terrible night and by morning they were resolved that, no matter how hard the journey might be, they would go back through the valley of rocks before the boy's sickness got worse. But the elder brother could not walk. His legs had turned into a thick green tail covered with scales. The only way the boys could travel was by taking turns carrying him across their shoulders. "Take me home," he cried as they climbed among the ragged rocks. "Please take me home!" And so they went along slowly and painfully until they came to another little lake formed, like the first one, by a waterfall that cascaded over the cliff.

"You must help me into the water," the boy urged them, even before they had put him down. "Please do as I ask and I won't bother you again, I promise. Just put me in the water."

Unwillingly, the two helped him into the water. Immediately he laughed and pulled free of them. Then with a leer he slithered off into the darkness of the water. All that night his brother and Anpao sat shivering beside the lake, unable to find enough wood to keep their fire burning, and listening to the elder brother splashing and leaping about in the black lake. They did not speak or look at each other. They waited silently for daylight.

When at last it was dawn, the sick boy giggled at them as he glided glistening from the water and slid effortlessly onto the shore.

"Ah," Anpao groaned, for his friend had been utterly transformed. Only his arms and his head were his own. The rest of his body was that of a giant green snake.

"Do not look so sad," said the snake-boy. He laughed, but his voice was almost gone, and when he spoke the sounds he made were gasps and hisses. "Let us continue on our way," he hissed. "Don't be afraid. I know exactly what I am doing," he said confidently.

So the others, horrified and dazed, followed Snake Boy, who slithered among the rocks with ease. His body was very sleek and long, and he hissed and giggled as he hurried along.

When the day was almost over, they reached a vast river at the end of the valley of rocks.

"Here is my home," Snake Boy hissed, as he slid into the water. "But stay here with me a little longer, my friends, because there are things I must tell you before you go. Do not mourn for me or cry for me. Brother, when you return to our village you must tell our people that we must accept whatever it is we are becoming. I have learned this and now I will be all right. Sometimes we grow up to be like everyone else, but sometimes we do not. People are always afraid of turning into something unusual, but they must not be afraid. We must be happy with whatever we are becoming. That is the way it is and that is the way it was intended to be."

With that, Snake Boy giggled happily and slipped out of sight. His brother called out to him and begged him not to leave them. He promised that he would find help—someone with such great power that he could change the snake-boy back into a boy. But there was no reply. Anpao stared out into the black lake. "Perhaps," he said, "he does not want to be a boy." And then they were silent.

The two friends paced the banks of the river all night, crying and offering prayers and peering into the darkness for a sign of Snake Boy, but he did not return to them. When the dawn was near, the two boys could remain awake no longer. Their day's journey and their hunger had weakened them, and finally they fell asleep by the river.

"Sheeeee..." came a voice. "Shsss-wake shsss-up! Shsss-wake shsss-up shsss-and shsss-look shsss-at shsss-me!"

Anpao jumped to his feet and stared across the river. Rising from the misty water was a gigantic serpent whose body was covered with luminous blue and green scales and whose head was crowned with twin horns. It was the most amazing sight Anpao had ever seen. The younger brother had also awakened and was crouching in fear of the vision in the black river.

"Do not be afraid, my brother. I am still your friend," the serpent hissed across the water.

"Yes, yes." The younger brother wept, as he slowly stood up. "I am not afraid and I still love you, my brother."

"Then do not weep. Be happy because I have finally found the place where I truly belong."

"It cannot be! How could this happen to you, my brother?"

"It is true, and you must accept it, and you must promise not to talk about it. You must tell our people that I am not dead. I am taking care of this great river. When you cross it you must think about me, and you must bring meat for me and drop it into the river. If you will do this whenever you cross this water, I will bless and protect you."

"I promise," said his brother, weeping. "I will tell them everything you have said."

"Now come to me," the great serpent hissed as he slithered over the water toward the shore. "I will not see you again, my little brother, and I want to kiss you good-by. Do not be afraid; I won't hurt you."

Reluctantly the younger brother crept toward the river's edge, and as Anpao watched in amazement, he put his arms around the giant snake's neck. Then the snake licked his face with its bright red, forked tongue.

For a moment Snake Boy looked intently, perhaps sadly, at Anpao and his brother. Then he vanished into the water.

The Sorceress

The bright yellow gourds faded with the end of summer, and the people of the village sat in the shade playing squaw-dice and speaking reverently of the fate of Snake Boy. Large metallic-looking flies buzzed about in the burning sunlight, and everywhere across the wide landscape the slender pods that dangled from dry bushes twisted slowly in the heat and then burst open, releasing countless airborne seeds.

Since the disappearance of Snake Boy, Anpao had remained in the lodge of his younger brother. Autumn and winter had passed. Spring rains had come and gone, and now the new summer was almost over. In the sunbaked village a celebration was under way in honor of the anniversary of the descent of Snake Boy into the great river. All the young men had assembled to sing and dance.

"Ah," the young brother of Snake Boy grunted discontentedly. "It is too hot to do anything but sit in the shade. Why don't you come and talk with us, Anpao? You never want to sit down. If you are not careful, you will wear off the soles of your feet." Everyone laughed, but Anpao would not sit with his friends. He stood staring off into the distance as he always did—as if he could hear and see something there which was invisible to everyone else. The sister of Snake Boy gazed at Anpao wherever he went. She rarely spoke to him, but her eyes always followed him, and she was never very far away from him. When she got up and strolled out to where Anpao was standing by himself, the young people smiled and pretended to concentrate on their game.

The girl was always self-conscious when she approached Anpao. For a long time she stood silently next to him and peered into the distance trying to see whatever it was he saw. She could see nothing, but Anpao could see many things. He gazed into the sunlit grass and the outstretched land so intently that he was not even aware that the girl was there. The Sun was dressing the edges of the evening with his finest plumage of fire. The burnished light streaked across the great plain, turning the tides of wind-tossed grass luminous and yellow. Birds leaped into flight and were pinned like darts of gold against the blazing sky.

Then the Sun drew his elegant robes around his shoulders and covered his head. He loomed momentarily as a glorious globe of russet light, pulsating on the horizon with his unfathomable power. If you looked upon him, you would be blinded—until he sank to his knees and washed his golden face in the river. Then, as his vibrance dimmed, Anpao could look upon him, until the Sun suddenly sailed away into the night where his wife, the Moon, awaited him impatiently.

In the coolness that followed the Sun's departure, the people came out from their lodges for the Giveaway ceremony. The old people stood proudly and offered the eloquent speeches which accompany ceremonial gift-giving. Then the songs began.

When it was Anpao's turn to dance everyone hurried to the dance ring to watch; he was a fine dancer and everyone greatly admired him. But no one admired Anpao as much as did the sister of Snake Boy. Her name was Amana, and she was so enchanted by him that she could think of nothing else.

When the dance ended, everyone honored Anpao and paid him compliments for the beauty of his dance. Amana wanted to speak to him, but so many young women surrounded him that she could not get near enough to be heard. So she decided that she would bring him a cool drink from the water hole. It was located on the far side of the encampment, and Amana knew that she would have to hurry if she were to bring Anpao the water before another girl did so. As she neared the well, she thought she saw the flutter of a skirt and a wisp of something in the air. But the fleeting shadow vanished into the darkness as Amana came near.

"Hello?" she called, but there was no reply. All was curiously silent, except for the distant voices of the people at the dance ring.

Amana quickly filled her water jug, peering into the darkness as she started back to the fire. She was a bit frightened, though she did not know what premonition possessed her. As she hurried along, she started and gasped. Before her was the glowing face of a very old woman. It was the strange one who lived alone in her tipi in the outermost circle of the camp. Amana glanced uneasily at the old woman, for the people spoke badly of her. She was very ugly and she sat silently by her fire, meticulously combing her long hair, looking aimlessly into the air with a dreamy smile on her wrinkled mouth. Amana nervously bade her "Good evening," but the old one paid no attention. She continued to comb her long black hair and smiled listlessly.

When Amana arrived at the dance ring where the fire burned brightly, she could see in the flickering light that the water in her jug was murky. But before she could throw it away, her brother caught sight of her. "Look here," he said, "Amana has brought some cool water." He took the jug and gave it to Anpao. As Anpao took a long drink, the Moon came out from behind a cloud. Amana felt a wind blow through the warm night, and then it was gone.

When Anpao awakened the next day, he told the brother of Snake Boy that he did not feel well.

"But, Anpao, my friend, you must rest and get better quickly. Tonight is the biggest dance of all and you have to dance better than ever!"

"But I can't even stand up. My leg hurts and there seems to be some kind of bruise on my calf."

"Let me take a look at it." Anpao stretched out on the grass and his friend inspected the injured leg. "That's very strange," he told Anpao. "There is a lump just under the skin, a round, dark lump. Perhaps you danced too hard last night. I've known some good dancers who danced too much and injured themselves. Maybe if I rub it for you and put cool water on the bruise it will be better for tonight."

But the pain did not go away and Anpao felt even worse by nightfall. "I will be all right," he reassured his friend. "You go along to the dance ring and I will paint myself and dress. Don't worry about me; I will be fine once I start dancing." His friend left him reluctantly and joined the people at the dance ring, where everyone had gathered for the biggest dance of the celebration.

The group dances and the Giveaways occupied most of the evening. Then, when the last Round Dance was over, everyone formed a big circle to watch the young men perform the fastest and most difficult dances. Amana sat with her brother and watched anxiously for Anpao. She smiled when she saw him stride into the dance ring, greeted by whoops of encouragement. He seemed to have recovered from his injury. When he waved to Amana and her brother she felt marvelous and proud, for everyone admired Anpao and wanted to be his friend.

Then the drumming began and the people fell silent. Anpao stood alone in the firelight, tall and handsome in his bright clan paint and elaborate regalia. He began with a slow dance with complex athletic steps, moving in a large circle while the people called out greetings to him. Amana thought he was dancing better than she had ever seen him dance before. Surely none of the other young men could possibly perform as well. But then Amana noticed something that frightened her: a shadow fluttered through the firelight and the Moon sailed mysteriously behind a dense cloud. Anpao was slowing down. He moved on the beat of the drum, but his legs moved with difficulty and his knees trembled. Amana glanced anxiously at her brother and could see by his expression that he had also noticed that something was going wrong.

"Ah! the fast dance!" the man next to Amana shouted gleefully, as the drums doubled the rhythm, going faster and faster.

For a moment Anpao's figure moved perfectly to the frantic beat, and his bright feathered costume blurred into an immense, luminous flower in the flickering of the fire. But then he stopped.

There, in the center of the dance ring, he suddenly froze and let out a fierce cry of pain. Amana was on her feet at once and with a sob she ran toward Anpao. Before she could reach him he had fallen to the ground.

All that night and the next day and the following night, Amana sat in the tipi where Anpao lay unconscious. "I think," whispered her brother, "that he will die, Amana." But Amana would not believe it. She angrily pushed her brother away and continued to massage Anpao's leg. Now and again he awakened briefly, but he didn't recognize any-one. He would try to sit up; then he would groan and pass out again.

On the fifth day, Amana began to fear that perhaps her brother was right . . . that Anpao would die. But she would not give in to death. Perhaps she was not powerful enough to help him. But if she could do nothing, surely there was someone with great enough healing power to save him! Amana urgently sought the help of the spirits, and sometimes, when she grew very tired toward morning, she would weep.

Then she remembered stories of a holy man who had helped many of the old people in the long-ago days with his great medicine. No young person had ever seen him, and even the old ones feared him and spoke his name in whispers. Though the stories of the holy man frightened Amana, she so desperately wanted to save Anpao's life that she decided to take him to the distant lodge of the great healer. She begged her brother to help her tie the strongest and biggest dogs to a travois on which she had made a bed of furs for Anpao. As soon as the two poles had been secured to the dogs and Anpao had been placed on the sling of hide she had stretched between the poles, Amana set off.

"You must not go, Amana," her brother had argued. "He is a good fellow, but he is not one of us and you are a fool to die for him. No one our age has ever gone to the mountain where the old man lives. You will never see your people again. You must stay here with me and we'll all do the best we can for Anpao."

"No," Amana said. "I know what I must do. I feel it is right and I must do it. Someone has put poison into the body of Anpao; that is what has happened to him. I must find a person who is more powerful than the poison, someone who can take it out. I know where I am going and what I must do. I promise you that I shall come back safely and that I will never leave the village again if you will allow me this once to help Anpao."

Her brother shook his head sadly, realizing that he

could do nothing to stop Amana. "You are just a foolish girl in love and you will die for it. But I cannot stop you, so go ahead and do what you must. I wish you safety and good spirits to help you. I have lost my only brother to the river and now I will lose my sister to the mountain."

"I am not lost," Amana said, as the large dogs barked and started toward the distant mountain. "This is a journey I must take, not only to save the life of Anpao, but to save my own life as well."

Amana knew exactly where she was going and so did the dogs. Deep within her heart there was a road and she knew it well, though she had never traveled it before.

When they arrived at the lodge, the holy man stood at the entrance as if he were expecting them. "You are late," he grumbled, without looking at Amana. "I am too old to be kept waiting. The hawk flies very high and the wind is good, but still you are late in coming. I am too old to be kept waiting."

Before Amana could say anything, the old man waved her away with an impatient gesture. She fell back in fear and the dogs cringed and their hair bristled as the old one stumbled blindly forward and gazed with dark eyes at Anpao.

"Ah," he grunted fiercely. "He is very nearly dead."

The holy man dropped to his knees and a great torrent of grief seized him and many tears fell from his old eyes.

"Ah," he wailed, "the world of his heart is already dark and eternal night waits like a wolf for him to lay down his bow. Ah, my son, listen now to the words of your father. You want to turn away from your journey and rest with your mother. But I will not let you go. Over the earth lodge many spirits sail . . . sail and drop down through the smoke hole. Flowers bend heavily on their stems. Everything wishes to sleep, but you must wake up. *Na-ho!* Do you hear me? Listen to the wind in the trees, my son. You must awaken now. I will find the poison in your leg and I will cut it out and then you must awake!"

The holy man shaded his eyes with an eagle feather and peered at Anpao's swollen leg. "There it is! I can see it!" Now the old one began brushing the swollen flesh with the feather, gathering all the evil into one terrible sore under the skin of Anpao's calf. Then the old man took a hollow animal horn in one hand and his stone knife in the other. He carefully cut into the evil and then he put the horn over the cut and began to suck at it. Three times he sucked at the wound and spit something into his palm that he quickly tossed into the fire. Three times the fire leaped up angrily to consume the poison. The last time the old man shouted, "I have it! I have it!"

The holy one shook his head slowly and held out his hand so Amana could see what was in his palm. There was a tiny knot of tangled black hairs. When Amana saw the hair she knew exactly what it was and how it had come to be in Anpao's leg. "The old woman is a sorceress!" she cried. "She did this to Anpao out of spite!"

"Ah, perhaps that is so. Perhaps it is so and perhaps it is not so. But now he is cured. And the old woman will die if she did this. She will die just as a bee must die when it stings us. So do not worry about the sorceress. Just go home, and by the time you reach your camp Anpao will be well again."

When Amana reached the village her brother came running out to meet her. Just as the holy man had promised, Anpao awoke and smiled as soon as the dogs dragged him to the entrance of the lodge.

"You are wiser than I am," the brother told Amana. "You have saved Anpao and now he will come and live with us and be your husband."

Amana cried out and covered her head and ran into the tipi while the young people laughed. Anpao, however, looked distressed.

"Anpao," Amana's brother exclaimed, "will you come and speak with my sister?"

"I cannot," Anpao said sadly. "Forgive me, but I cannot speak with her now. I must think about everything that has happened to me." When the brother frowned, Anpao took his arm gently and said, "Please, my friend, do not be unhappy. Tonight I will speak to Amana. I promise it."

But when the night had come, Anpao still could not speak. He stood at the edge of the village, staring off into the distance as he always did—as if he could hear and see something that was invisible to everyone else. Amana watched him from a distance for a long time and then she slowly approached and stood by his side.

"I cannot stay here," Anpao murmured, without looking at her. "And I cannot tell you why." They stood silently for a long time in the darkness, listening to the pine tinder popping in the distant campfire.

"Forgive me," he said quietly, as he turned to her. "Even when I hear the voices of your village and see the smiles of your people, still there is something that I cannot find here. I do not know exactly what it is. The fire is warm and the land is good, but inside me there is another land. When I dream, I do not dream of this place, Amana, but of another land. When I hear singing, it is not the song you sing. When I search in the dark, I find nothing familiar. I cannot see what it is I am looking for. I only catch glimpses of someone in the distance. A face in the smoke. A voice in the silence of the morning. But as the days go by I grow weary. I have come so far and I have found so very little, Amana. I have searched so long that it is no longer clear to me where it is I am going or why. I have come so far that I have become my journey and my journey has become me. Without it I am nothing. When I pause I forget who I am or why I exist.

"I cannot find myself among your lodges or among your people, Amana. I cannot stay here and I cannot tell you exactly why. If I stop now, I will become a tree among all these trees. Forgive me, but I cannot be a tree, Amana. Do you see how they pull at their roots and shake their branches at the sky? I cannot be a tree, Amana. They are prisoners of this forest, growing taller and taller and trying to grow above one another, trying to see all the vast world beyond the forest which they can never travel. And so, do you understand, Amana, why I cannot stay here with you?"

She gazed at him for a moment and then smiled rather weakly and touched his shoulder. "Yes, Anpao, I understand. Like me, you have a road in your heart. For you, Anpao, that road leads away." She covered her face with her hand

and stepped back slowly, gazing for a long moment into Anpao's face. Then she turned and ran away.

The Moon came from behind a cloud and smiled a dreadful, pallid smile. Silently she combed her long black hair and sang a little song to pleasure herself.

Anpao and the Animals

Anpao had traveled very far, crossing the vast river where Snake Boy lived and coming at last to the endless red desert in the South where the Ancient Ones had lived when they first emerged from the underworld.

Day after day he walked under the Sun, who watched him intently and threw down his ferocious blessings. Anpao was hungry, for he had nothing to eat but seeds of the wild plants which grew in dry clumps in the vast desert land. When it was evening and the air became cool, Anpao ground the seeds between two flat stones. Then, adding just a bit of the precious water he carried in a gourd, he made a gruel, which didn't taste very good but kept him alive.

Each night Anpao stopped in exhaustion as the evening's breeze came across the desert, and each night he made camp and slept under the torrent of stars that brightened the great sky above the wasteland. He listened to the desert mice scampering among the dry roots and to the owl's soft conversation about the stars and the universe beyond the stars. Then he dreamed of food and of Ko-ko-mik-e-is.

In the morning the great red ants were the first to emerge into the abrupt blaze of the Sun as he came over the horizon. Soon the ants were hard at work building, always building, their monumental ant worlds.

One evening when Anpao was about to make camp, he saw smoke rising in the distance. Though he was very tired, he decided to seek out the strangers in the hope that they might share their food with him. He walked for a long distance, following the wisps of smoke which circled in the failing daylight. Once it was dark he gave up, realizing he could not possibly reach the strangers' camp without light. But just then he heard the distant voices of people resounding over the utter silence of the desert night. Cautiously, Anpao followed the sounds.

When at last he came upon the camp, he walked silently toward the fire, hoping that whoever was there might see that he came in peace. But instead of welcoming him, the people in the camp whimpered and clutched one another. They were the skinniest, most miserable people Anpao had ever seen. They crouched on the ground and gazed at him while they continued to whimper and moan.

"I am called Anpao," he told them, but they only trembled. Then suddenly they darted into the darkness beyond their fire's glow. "Please!" Anpao exclaimed. "I am very hungry. Will you share your food with me?"

There was no reply from the darkness.

Anpao sat close to the meager fire, for the night on the high desert was very cold. Then he waited. The sky darkened and the wind turned colder. Anpao could hear the moans of the people who huddled beyond the fire's light in the cold night. But still they would not return to their camp. They had run off and abandoned all their possessions, their food, and the beautiful baskets in which they kept their belongings. Anpao could not recall seeing more finely made baskets anywhere. But these people didn't seem to know how to defend their camp. Instead, they left everything and cringed somewhere out in the darkness of the desert, leaving Anpao to help himself to anything he wanted.

"You are fools!" he shouted into the night. "I do not mean to harm anybody. All I want is a bit of your food. Do you hear what I am saying? Do you hear? Ah, but you are fools!"

Anpao became so annoyed by the lack of hospitality of these fearful people that he decided to have a bit of their food. He ate a little dried meat and a few of the sweet seeds that were kept in the baskets but would not take any more of their food despite his terrible hunger. To take something that was not given was to behave like a savage.

"Ah!" he grumbled, crouching by the fire and trying to sleep. "You people are fools to be afraid of a stranger." Then he closed his eyes.

"Psst!" came a voice. "Psssst!"

"What!" shouted Anpao, jumping to his feet and staring about him anxiously. It was utterly dark now, for the fire had gone out, and he could see nothing but two little glowing embers where the fire had been. "Who is it?"

"May I come near?" the little voice asked.

"Yes, yes," Anpao whispered. "You may come near, but I have nothing but water to give you."

"Only water? Well, you are poor indeed if all you have is water," the stranger said as he walked into the glow of the embers. "Very poor indeed." He dropped a bundle of twigs onto the orange coals and almost instantly the fire sprang up.

The stranger was a raven. He had a handsome bow in his parfleche and a quiver full of finely made arrows on his back. Without speaking a word, he put these beautiful weapons down near the fire. Then he took a large bundle wrapped in rawhide from under his arm and this too he put next to the fire.

"Do you live in this camp?" Anpao asked.

"That is exactly what I was about to ask you," said Raven.

"No," Anpao assured him. "I have been traveling for many many days. I hoped the people of this camp might be generous to me, but they simply ran off and they will not come back no matter how often I offer them my friendship."

"Well, that is reasonable," Raven said thoughtfully, throwing back his feathered robe and scratching his leg. "These desert people can be very timid. They will run off and leave all their possessions rather than face an enemy. You are probably the first person I have ever met who did not run away as soon as I approached, so obviously you do not come from the desert."

"No, I am not from this land," Anpao explained. "I come from a mountainous place in the North and . . ." But Raven was not listening. Without saying a word he arose, drew his cloak closed, and walked into the darkness. Anpao watched after him silently for a long time. Perhaps Raven was going to fetch more wood for the fire. But he did not return.

The fire was growing dim once again, and Anpao was afraid to go to sleep. He wanted to find some firewood but he was unexplainably frightened of the immense darkness that surrounded him, and he would not venture beyond the fire's dismal light. He sat down and gazed at the wonderful bow and the quiver of arrows and the bundle that Raven had left by the fire. What could be in the bundle? Perhaps it was food. Perhaps it was powerful medicine that belonged to Raven. For a long time Anpao resisted the temptation to open the bundle, but finally he decided to take a peek at whatever was inside.

"Ah!" he exclaimed, when he opened the rawhide and found a strange meat and many lumps of fat. "Ah, but this is very good!" he said happily, as he nibbled at a bit of the meat. It was like nothing he had ever eaten. And as he ate, strange things began to happen to him. He became stronger and filled with enormous energy and power. Obviously this meat of Raven's was very special.

Just when Anpao was cautiously wrapping what was left of the meat and fat back into the bundle, Raven stepped into the firelight and cackled. He knew at once what had happened. "KAAAAAAAAAAAH!" he shouted in anger. Anpao fell back and wiped his mouth with a guilty gesture. Before he had a chance to apologize for behaving so badly, Raven snatched up his possessions and flew away to the East.

The shy people of the camp, who had crouched all night

in the cold and dark, saw Raven fly away and they unfolded their membranous wings and darted into the air in wild flights, following Raven into the darkest of the desert night.

It was not until the next night, while Anpao slept and the fire burned low, that the people finally crept back into their camp. They peered at the sleeping young man with their enormous, bulging eyes and twitched their little mouse ears fretfully as they approached. Their cloaks were so thin that they were transparent, making countless tiny veins visible. Their legs were so short that they could barely stand or walk. And they trembled with fear as they ogled the stranger.

Gradually they gained courage and hobbled forward, holding their tangled skin robes in their bony little arms, which they crossed on their furry chests.

One of the people approached Anpao and sniffed his long hair. At that moment he awoke and sat up abruptly. The people tumbled to the ground and staggered toward the darkness to escape. Some of them leaped into jagged flight, darting at the fire and then soaring back into the darkness in a frenzied, zigzag maneuver.

Then suddenly the largest of the people landed next to Anpao and screeched in what is considered among the desert dwellers a very friendly manner. Anpao, however, thought he was being attacked and shouted in fear, "What do you want here?"

The creature laughed because he had never been able to frighten anyone before. "Did I really scare you?" he asked politely.

"Well . . . a bit," Anpao admitted.

"Hmmmm," the other said. "You are a foolish-looking creature. I have never seen such a person. . . . If you could only see yourself!" he said, and giggled. "Afraid of a bat! Why should you possibly be afraid of us?"

"Because," Anpao muttered in annoyance, "you are so ugly!"

"Ah, well," the bat said philosophically. "That is quite another matter, it seems to me. Yes, we bats are rather ugly, that is true enough. I don't think even the prettiest of us would disagree with you on that subject. But do you really think we are dangerous just because we are ugly? You are a very stupid creature if that is how you think."

Anpao felt embarrassed because this ugly bat was obviously very wise. "It is true," Bat continued in a considering tone, "that your kind of people are often quite handsome and tall. We bats would not dispute that. But why are you so afraid of things that are ugly? I can think of many people who are beautiful but who are also very dangerous. I can think of berries and toadstools which are quite handsome but are also very poisonous. However, with ugly things it is quite a different matter. Most of the ugly things in the world are so busy being ugly that they don't really have time to bother anybody. Let me give you an example . . ."

"I have heard enough," Anpao barked at the talkative bat. "I am sorry . . . all right? I admit I made a mistake. It is true, you are not dangerous and it was foolish for me to be afraid. Now the only thing I fear is that you might talk me to death!" At this Bat and Anpao laughed.

Hearing the laughter, all the bats gradually took courage and came back to their camp where they carefully inspected Anpao to see for themselves that he was not as dangerous as he looked. Then they snuggled in their membranous robes and gathered around the fire where they sang this beautiful night song:

> "In the night
> the rain comes down,
> and at the edge of the earth
> there is a wound
> and there is a sound.
> Down beyond the desert it slowly rumbles;
> it is the song of the night."

After the song and after the bat-people shared their seeds, roots, and fat grubs with Anpao, they told him that they had followed Raven to his hiding place. Anpao was pleased by this news and asked them if they would show him where Raven's lodge was located, for that clever fellow possessed a powerful meat and Anpao admitted that he wanted to take it from him.

The small bats were unwilling to leave the safety of their camp, but the biggest among them, the talkative one who had become Anpao's friend, agreed to lead him to the place where Raven lived.

"I am very grateful to you," Anpao said, as he lay down to sleep and dream of the powerful meat of Raven.

"That is another thing which I do not understand about you people who are so handsome and tall," Bat said. "You are always grateful and you are always spiteful and you are always saying one thing but doing another, and sometimes I think that you are the most dangerous animals of all. Now tell me something: why are you so afraid of all the other animals if you are the one that is actually the most dangerous?"

But Anpao was already asleep. The large bat grunted in dismay, covering his head and mumbling about the vanity of people who are beautiful. Then he too went to sleep.

Anpao had to travel at night, for his guide was blinded by sunlight. In the day he slept and in the night he traveled across the red desert. After many nights of walking over the endless sand, Bat and Anpao came to a lone towering rock that rose out of the flatland. Long before they could see any living things on this solitary mount, they could hear distant voices coming across the desert. The sounds were made by hundreds of fierce ravens, who had their home upon this holy mountain.

When the Sun arose and Bat climbed into his cocoon of wings to sleep, dangling upside down from a branch, Anpao hid behind a thorny tree and tried to find the raven who had visited him. He was nowhere to be found. The other ravens flew above him in large swooping circles, cawing and screaming but saying nothing that Anpao could understand.

"These ravens have ravenous appetites, and that means they have to make a cooking fire soon," Anpao was thinking, as he searched the small caves along the base of the mountain looking for the ashes of old fires. "Ahuh!" he whispered, when he saw a large circle of charred wood and ashes. "This is where they must do their cooking, but where do they hide the food they cook?"

Anpao had never before tasted meat quite like the kind he had stolen from Raven. No other food had ever made him feel so strong and powerful. He knew that if he were to succeed in climbing to the house of the Sun, he would have to be as strong as he had felt after eating the meat from Raven's bundle. So he decided to hide behind a rock and watch until the ravens came down to cook.

Anpao waited patiently all night and all the next day. The ravens swooped over his hiding place, cawing loudly and diving down toward the spot where they usually built their cooking fire, but they didn't make a fire and they didn't reveal where their precious food was hidden.

That night, when Bat awakened, Anpao told him that he was discouraged and could not wait any longer for the ravens to disclose the source of the rich meat. Bat stretched as he listened to Anpao. Then he sat down and sighed. "Well, it seems a shame to have come all this way and not find what we are looking for."

"These ravens are too smart for us," Anpao answered. "Whatever this meat might be, the ravens are not going to let us find out their secret."

"But what if we pretend to leave and I fly far ahead while you hide? Perhaps that might fool them."

Anpao was not convinced that the trick would work, but Bat talked on and on, insisting that they try to fool the ravens. So Anpao put his possessions into a bundle and, with Bat flying ahead of him, he marched away from the camp of the ravens. When they had traveled a considerable distance and the ravens no longer followed high above them, Anpao and Bat hid in the brush. "Now we can fool them!" Bat screeched happily. "If we sneak back to their camp, we can see what they are up to."

So, moving very cleverly among the bushes, they hurried back toward the raven encampment. When they were close enough to see the campfire, they hid behind a boulder and peeked over its edge.

The ravens had come down to their camp and were flocked around their cooking fire, chattering about all sorts of gossip they had heard while flying over the countryside.

Then Anpao saw the oldest and largest of the ravens walk to the middle of the circle where the fire was made. He brushed away the ashes of the old fire with both his hands and gradually uncovered a large flat stone, which was fitted into the ground under the campfire. Several of the strongest ravens stepped forward and, with a good deal of grunting and puffing, they managed to lift the stone until it stood on its side. Now the five largest ravens disappeared beneath the stone. They didn't come back for a long while, but when they did reappear they drove a large animal up through the hole and into the camp of the ravens. Then they chased the animal and shot many arrows into its sides. Finally the great creature fell dead. The entire encampment of ravens shouted happily and descended upon the carcass with sharp stone knives.

"So that is how they get their special meat!" Bat clucked.

"But what kind of a creature is it? I have never seen anything like it."

"They called it buffalo . . . and that is its name," Bat explained. "What it is I cannot tell you, but it is the power of its meat that lets ravens fly so far and so high."

"Well, whatever it is, I know that I want to get some of it. The ravens have no right to keep these buffaloes secret."

"Perhaps you are right and perhaps you are wrong, Anpao, but regardless of that I think you are going to have a hard time stealing the secret from the ravens."

"We were smart enough to fool them this far. Why not at least try to get down into that hole and find out where these great creatures come from?"

"I am not a big fellow like you, and I don't want any trouble with the ravens. I tell you what, I will wait here. You can try to steal a buffalo if that is really what you want to do. As for me, I am contented with the grubs I eat and have no wish to chase buffaloes."

Anpao agreed to go alone, so when all the ravens were busy storing their freshly cut meat in their tipis, he crept toward the opening in the fireplace. He took one cautious look around and then quickly leaped into the hole.

Below the ravens' camp there was a beautiful world, in which many handsome animals happily grazed in a great unbroken sea of grass. Of all the animals, those called buffaloes were the most numerous; their great herds of many colors roamed peacefully in every direction. Of the countless buffaloes, four were the largest and seemed to be the chiefs. Anpao carefully approached these leaders. He took an eagle feather from his hair and slowly put it into the mouth of the chief white buffalo.

The buffalo shook his head. "This feather is not for me," he said. "You want my brother who is the chief of the black buffaloes."

Anpao looked at the white buffalo chief suspiciously but decided that he was perhaps telling the truth, so he carefully approached the black buffalo chief and placed the feather in his mouth. But the black buffalo shook his head.

"No, no," he snorted politely. "You have not come for me. Go back to my brother. He is the greatest of all animals, but he is too modest to tell you so."

Immediately Anpao rushed back to the white buffalo chief and placed the feather in his mouth. "I am no longer fooled, chief of the white buffaloes," he said. "I know your power now. You are truly the chief of all animals and the most sacred of them all." The buffalo could not deny it, and so he held the feather between his teeth and followed Anpao to the surface of the world. All the other animals, seeing the white buffalo chief leaving the beautiful world below, lifted their heads and silently followed. Every kind of animal that had never before lived in the world followed Anpao and the white buffalo chief.

It took Anpao a long time to find his way back to the world, and by the time Anpao and the animals came through the hole it was night and the ravens were all asleep. Luckily their cooking fire had cooled, so Anpao and the animals could pass quietly through the ashes and out of the encampment.

As the last animal climbed through the hole in the earth, it slipped and fell, awakening one of the ravens, who immediately jumped to his feet and tried to push the stone back over the hole. But it was too late; all the animals had escaped.

"KAAAAAAAH!" the raven screeched. "You have won! The animals belong to your people now, you wicked creature! But whenever you kill any of them, you must always leave the eyes for the ravens. That is very little to ask for so great a gift."

Then all the ravens rose into the air and loudly lamented their lost secret.

Anpao stood among the herds of marvelous new animals, watching the angry ravens swoop overhead. Then, bidding his friend Bat good-by, he started his long journey once again, walking toward the distant forest. He walked for many days, with all the new animals following after him as tamely as though they were sheep.

When at last they reached a small camp, the buffaloes scattered in search of tender grass, and Anpao tried to rouse someone from whom he could ask for food and water. But the village seemed vacant and there was no one Anpao could tell about the new animals and their powerful meat.

While Anpao searched the lodges, a deer, the most beautiful of the new animals, began to nibble the grass that covered an earthen lodge. In a moment an old woman scrambled from the lodge and shouted fiercely at the deer. She picked up a stick from the fire and thrust the flaming end at the deer's face. The ash brushed the frightened animal's nose, so that ever since deer have had a white mark on their faces.

"Don't be so damn friendly!" the old woman shouted at the deer. "Stay away from people from now on! Just use your nose and you will know when you are near us. Then run away if you know what's good for you!"

The deer looked at the angry woman in dismay and then bounded from the camp, and all the other animals followed him.

"You are a very stupid woman," Anpao said sternly. "You have destroyed the friendship between the new animals and people. Now you will have to chase after them and beg them to sacrifice themselves to you."

"Can that be true?" The old woman groaned as she looked after the fleeing animals. "Then I have indeed been foolish. Please forgive me, and please," she begged, "ask the new animals to come back!"

"It is too late," Anpao told her, putting his bundle on his back. "If the animals are not welcome here, I will not stay. I will follow them to a safer place to stay for the night. Yes, I think perhaps Bat was right after all: the world of people is far too dangerous."

Anpao Brings the Corn

The enormous Moon watched over the new animals that Anpao had brought into the world. Among them were also new people, like none Anpao had seen. Though they were strange in appearance, their eyes shone with great power. And though these strangers could not speak as other people spoke, they perfectly understood the world and all that was in it. They understood green. They laughed at running water. They watched the grass grow, and they climbed effortlessly among cobwebs. Wherever the animals went, they also went, for they understood every living thing. And their power was so great that they could stop the cascades of the waterfalls. They could halt the flight of birds in midair and turn the vast sky into a light-flooded crystal.

These new people had short hairless tails, large eyes, and very long ears. At night when they slept they lay down on one of their ears and covered themselves with the other one. In the morning they emerged from these ear-beds and stretched their webbed hands and feet. Then they scratched their heads, which were covered with pale green moss. After eating some of the rich buffalo fat, they spoke in signs to all the animals.

They told them that the way back into the world

below was forever sealed and that all the new animals now belonged in the world of Anpao and his people. At first the new animals were in a forlorn state, deeply mourning the loss of their perfect world. Then slowly they began to explore the forests and the meadows. They cautiously sniffed and touched the trees and the grass and they gazed intently at Anpao.

"Is he an evil one or is he a good one?" one animal asked another.

For a long time there was no reply. Then one small creature ventured very close to Anpao and looked into his face. "I think he is good despite the fact that he looks just like all the others."

"Nonsense!" barked a man and a woman. "His people are bad and so is he!"

Anpao had not noticed these two strangers before, for they had been the very last to come from the world below. Their heads were covered with hoods that blew loosely around their shoulders in the wind. In their waxen hands these two people held all the power of the new people. They were Sorcerers who controlled all that is good and all that is bad.

"You do not know me—why have you spoken against me?" Anpao protested.

"We know your people and we detest them. Didn't your people drive the animals away? No, we want nothing to do with them. We must live in your world, but we will live with the new animals as far away as possible from all your haughty brothers."

"If you are going to be cruel to my people, then you

will find out very soon that they will not want you in their world," Anpao said flatly.

The Sorcerers laughed. "You are not the white buffalo chief—how dare you speak for the animals? And if you are speaking only for your own people, then let me tell you this. They will not chase us away! No, indeed, they will want us to stay. Do you see how we hold our hands clutched under our armpits? Do you see? In each hand we hold all the seeds of your world. If your people do not behave, we shall suck the life out of all the seeds and destroy your world of people. Nothing will grow, and your kind will starve to death. Even the new animals that you brought into your world will die."

The animals became anxious when they heard the Sorcerers' words and hid from them, climbing trees, leaping behind boulders, and galloping into the open meadow.

"I am not afraid of you," Anpao said, standing his ground. "So do not make threats! Tell me what you want of my people."

Again the Sorcerers laughed. "We want to live among you."

"And what will you give my people in exchange?"

"We have precious things," the Sorcerers whispered. "We will give all of these things to your people and make them powerful."

"And what must we do in order to be given these things? Must we do more than let you live among us?" Anpao asked cautiously.

"That was what we first offered in exchange for many

precious things, but you were haughty and you insulted us. Now we want more!"

"But what is it that you want now?"

"A boy and a girl. You must give up two of your people's children. When you give us the children, the seeds will be yours and the world of people will be bountiful," one of the Sorcerers said with a vague smile.

"But why do you need two of us?" Anpao asked.

The Sorcerers laughed and whispered to each other. Then the woman grinned unpleasantly and said, "So that they may die."

"What?"

"If they do not die, the rain will never come again and the seeds will wither and turn to dust."

"But I have no children," Anpao pleaded. "If you are really Sorcerers, you know very well that I have no children. I have only myself."

Again the Sorcerers whispered to each other and then turned to Anpao with smiles. "You have forgotten that you also have Ko-ko-mik-e-is!" they said and giggled. "Yes, indeed, you and she will do just fine!" They shrieked with delight, crouching down as they laughed and hopped from one foot to the other.

"Why must you destroy us? Must you really destroy Ko-ko-mik-e-is and me? Please, tell me, why do you do this when I have tried so hard to bother no one?"

"Be silent!" the Sorcerers shouted. "You could have had everything if you had not been so haughty! You rejected us before you knew us!"

"Ah," Anpao sighed. "Then it is done. You must do what you must do."

At this the Sorcerers came forward and spoke seriously to Anpao. "Then you must do exactly what we tell you to do. First you must lie down on the ground and you must remove all thoughts from your mind except for one thing: the heart of Ko-ko-mik-e-is! Do you understand? Are you ready? Now do as we have told you. Lie down quickly and empty your mind of all things but the heart of Ko-ko-mik-e-is. And as you see her heart you must tell us exactly what it is that you are thinking," the Sorcerers whispered into Anpao's ear as he sank into a dream.

"I am thinking," he murmured, "that I love Ko-ko-mik-e-is very much. I am thinking that she is the voice inside of me that takes me on my long journey. I am thinking that she is the place where my journey began and the place where it will end. She is the one familiar being in a world filled with strangers. She is within me, but I cannot find her."

"That is good," the Sorcerers told him. "Now touch the scar on your face and think of the Ko-ko-mik-e-is who is inside of you."

As Anpao put his fingers to his face, the ground beneath him groaned like a woman in labor. Furrows of rich soil opened beneath him and a wind blew the strong scent of pollen across his body. Gradually a body of light took shape inside his own body. As this luminous being grew and became solid, it could not remain within Anpao's flesh, for there was not enough space within him. The body of light slowly turned into skin and bones. Anpao twisted and panted under the tremendous weight of this new body, which bloated his veins and flesh. He arched his back and moaned as he labored to exhale the luminous figure. Little by little he pressed it out of himself, sobbing and trembling from an intense stinging in his blood.

"*Kyi!*" he shouted, and collapsed.

When Anpao opened his eyes, he could see Ko-ko-mik-e-is lying asleep just beside him. She was more beautiful than all the beautiful things he had seen during his long journey. She glistened like a newborn child and she smelled as sweet as a new flower. Anpao wanted to speak to her but he could not speak. He wanted to tell her that he had tried to ask the Sun's permission to marry her, but the journey had been too long and too difficult. He wanted to explain that the world was full of great powers, and he could not find the strength to overwhelm them and reach his journey's end. He wanted to tell Ko-ko-mik-e-is that he was sorry to have failed, but he could not form words and he could not make gestures. He could only look at Ko-ko-mik-e-is helplessly, knowing that he and she must be given to the Sorcerers. And so he turned his eyes away and he wept.

As his tears rolled from his cheeks and fell upon the ground, the sky blazed suddenly and there came a great thunder. Anpao's father, the Sun, was stung by each tear that fell from his son's eyes. In a fiery rage the Sun began beating furiously at the roof of the world, trying to drive the Sorcerers away. But his wife, the Moon, would not allow him to save his son. Anpao begged for pity from the Moon. He pleaded for the life of Ko-ko-mik-e-is. But the Moon turned away and called to her husband.

The Sorcerers leaned over the two young people. Anpao

wanted to shout, but he could make no sound. For a moment he caught sight of their perfectly oval white faces, which were hidden behind the hoods. He looked into their perfectly empty eyes, which reflected his own face back at him like the surface of a pool. Then long white fingers came out from under their cloaks and touched Ko-ko-mik-e-is and Anpao over their hearts and shot their ferocious emptiness into the young bodies. Instantly Anpao and Ko-ko-mik-e-is died.

The Sun, overwhelmed with grief, shouted curses at his jubilant wife and covered his face, leaving the world in a terrible darkness.

The new people crept from their hiding places and stared at the bodies of Anpao and Ko-ko-mik-e-is. For a long time it was more silent in the world than it had been since before the days when Old Man had created something out of nothing. Then a sound began to arise. The animals cried their wildest cries of grief. The white buffalo chief stamped his great hoofs so hard that Thunder came. The birds screamed so fiercely that the flowers closed their petals and turned brown. The sky raged, and Lightning, gone mad with grief, tore her glistening hair and screeched as she raced wildly across the sky.

The animals wept such torrents of tears that it rained four days and four nights, soaking the graves of Anpao and Ko-ko-mik-e-is. On the fifth day the earth began to rumble, and into the sky the Sun unfolded a vast canopy of gold, which showered the earth with life. Then came a great wind and suddenly Anpao and Ko-ko-mik-e-is rose up from their graves like saplings in spring.

"Ko-ko-mik-e-is!" Anpao shouted in joy.

For just a moment the beautiful girl wavered in the air like smoke, then she turned into yellow light and vanished. Where she had stood, the ground was soft, and from the rich black soil a plant sprouted and grew quickly into a tall, very green stalk. When this plant, which no one had ever seen before, was taller than the tallest of men, leaf-covered fruit appeared one by one in its armpits.

"Ah!" the animals exclaimed, when the Sorcerers stepped forward majestically and picked the fruit and pulled back the thick green husk.

"What is this fruit?" Anpao asked.

"It is called corn," the Sorcerers said. "Come and taste it."

Anpao ate some of the yellow kernels. "How good it is!"

The people and the animals also wanted to taste the mysterious corn and they crowded around the tall stalks waiting for more of the fruit to appear. Soon they were passing great armfuls of the sweet corn among all the people and all the animals. The corn and the fat of the buffalo were the gifts of the World-Below-the-World.

Everyone was so happy eating and singing and dancing that no one realized that the Sorcerers had disappeared.

"Ah!" all the animals and people exclaimed. "Where have the Sorcerers gone? And how can we thank them?"

Everyone put aside the new food and they all hurried in every direction searching for the Sorcerers. They called out to one another until their voices grew very distant. "Has anyone found the Sorcerers?" they shouted back and forth. But no one succeeded in finding them.

Just when Anpao was about to give up the search, he looked up into a tree and was astonished to see the two Sorcerers smiling down at him. They were sitting on the highest branches, looking down on the frenzied activity below. They laughed and, for the first time, they pushed back their hoods and completely revealed their faces. Anpao stared at them in surprise. Though he was certain he had never seen people quite like the Sorcerers, they were somehow familiar to him. They didn't look like the other people Anpao had known in his life. They didn't have long tails, or fur coats, or feathers. They were very smooth, except for the hair on the top of their heads, and they had only two legs and two arms, which were much shorter than their legs. Their hands had fingers and their feet had toes. They were very strange-looking beings. Occasionally Anpao had caught sight of a similar kind of face reflected in pools but, other than such glimpses, he had never seen anybody who looked like these amazing Sorcerers.

"Why are you staring at us?" they asked him, with grins on their unusual faces. "Don't you trust us now? Don't you believe in our power?"

"Oh, yes," Anpao whispered meekly. "Yes, I do."

"Then why are you frightened of us?"

"I am not frightened . . . I was only wondering . . ."

"What were you wondering?"

"I was wondering if the beautiful girl I saw lying next to me was *really* Ko-ko-mik-e-is."

The Sorcerers laughed very hard, making the tree shake. "*Really?*" the Sorcerers mocked. "Don't you know that *everything* is real?"

Anpao didn't know what to say to them. Again the Sorcerers laughed.

"Your people must sleep in order to have dreams and you always have the same question: *Is it real?* Your eyes and your brains have made prisoners of each other." Again the Sorcerers shook the tree with their laughter. "Your people have many possessions, but in dreams you are very poor."

As the Sorcerers laughed, more and more leaves fell from the tree. They laughed harder and harder until such a storm of leaves fell around Anpao that he could see nothing in the torrent. When at last the leaves settled to the ground, the tree was entirely bare. Fall had come and the wind was full of scarlet leaves. Nothing was left on the tree except the Sorcerers' abandoned robes and hoods.

Anpao peered incredulously at the bare tree. "*Ayeee!*" he shouted, turning to find himself staring into the eyes of a stranger. "Who are you and where did you come from?" he exclaimed. "Are you one of the Sorcerers?"

"Of course not," said the man indignantly. "Just look at me, you fool: I am one of the people you brought from the World-Below-the-World. Can't you tell from my long ears and my . . . Oh!" The man stopped with a flabbergasted cry, for when he touched his ears he found that they had been cleverly clipped off. And when he touched his tail he found that it too was gone. Even the moss had vanished from his head. "Ah!" he cried. "What have those Sorcerers gone and done to us now!"

It was true: the Sorcerers had clipped the tails and trimmed the ears of all the people on earth. "They have played a terrible trick on us!" the people complained. "We must find those nasty Sorcerers and demand that they put us back the way we were!"

But they couldn't find the Sorcerers anywhere. They shouted and they yelled and they fussed and pouted, but the Sorcerers did not answer. It seemed as though they had vanished for good.

Now everyone was very angry. Except Anpao . . . he sat under the leafless tree and laughed. "You are a total fool!" the people snapped at him as they hurried away. "What is so funny about our being turned into such ugly creatures! Now we have no ears and we have lost our handsome tails! We are just as ugly as you are!"

Long after the people had gone, Anpao continued to laugh, for he understood something that no one else understood. The Sorcerers had not vanished at all. They had done something extremely clever. They had simply remade all the people into their own image so they could safely hide among people without anybody ever realizing it. Ever since that day Sorcerers have secretly lived among men, unrecognized because they look just like other people. So no one ever knows if he has met one of the Sorcerers who came from the World-Below-the-World. They are the powerful ones still— the ones who hold in their hands all the seeds of things not yet born into our world.

Anpao and Coyote

Anpao awakened early and collected his few possessions. After saying good-by to the people and the animals from the World-Below-the-World, he turned to the Sun who smiled at him.

"Sun," Anpao chanted happily, "rise slowly and wait for me. I have soft feet like my mother and cannot climb as fast as you can climb the blue steps of the sky. Wait for me, my father."

But the Sun was the Sun and could not wait ... not even for his own child. And though Anpao hurried, the Sun eluded him.

Exhausted and hungry, Anpao reached a river and made camp on the bank. The wolves came to visit him and night birds flew overhead. He bathed in the cold water and he ate dried buffalo meat from his sack of possessions. Then he lay down and closed his eyes. He tried to recall how beautiful Ko-ko-mik-e-is had been when he saw her lying beside him in the ceremony that brought the corn. It made him feel very good and very sensual to gaze at the Ko-ko-mik-e-is who was in his mind.

"I go among girls and I see them all," Anpao sang

gently, as the wolves curled up beside him. "But I only like
the one I walked with first. My eyes are open for her and I
look at all the other girls as though I were just dreaming.
Perhaps Ko-ko-mik-e-is is dreaming of me, too."

The night was growing very cold and Anpao asked the
wolves to help him find firewood. They reluctantly got up
and, taking their stone axes, went into the thicket in search
of branches to build a large bonfire. They put more and
more wood on the fire until it blazed marvelously and threw
its reflection over the surface of the rolling river. Anpao sat
down in the warmth and gazed into the dance of the orange
and yellow and red fire-people. Then he curled up among the
wolves.

But still he could not sleep. All he could do was lie
awake in dreams of Ko-ko-mik-e-is. So again he began to
sing. "Whenever I am sleeping, I dream of my love for you.
Whenever I lie on my back in my camp, I lie on the pain
of your love, Ko-ko-mik-e-is. Whenever I walk and wherever
I journey, I step on the pain of your love. I fall asleep in the
starlit clearing of your forehead and I dream of a thousand
buffaloes that want to die for your love."

Puffp!

"What is that!" The wolves ran away in fear, and the
birds vanished.

Puffp!

"Ah!" Anpao cried out again, leaping to his feet and
searching the darkness. "What is that?" Whatever it was that
made such a strange sound must be something really terrible
to have frightened the wolves and the birds.

Puffp!

There it was again. "Who are you and what do you want from me?"

Nothing.

"Come close to the fire so I can see you!" Anpao shouted.

Puffp! Puffp! Puffp!

"Please," came a voice, "do not hurt me. I mean no harm. It's only me, Farting Boy."

Slowly a boy crept into the fire's light. He had a bow and a quiver of arrows in one hand and in the other a target. He seemed perfectly harmless, except that whenever he took a step he made a funny noise: *Puffp! Puffp!*

"May I warm myself at your fire?" he asked politely.

"Yes, of course, you are welcome. But, tell me, what is that you have in your hands?"

"Oh, these are my favorite things, my bow and my arrows and my target. The light is good here—so let me show you the game I play to amuse myself."

"Is it safe—this game of yours?" Anpao asked.

"Yes, of course it is. Watch." So after the boy had warmed his hands, he stood in the center of the clearing on the river's bank and threw the target into the air. Whenever he threw the target he would *puffp!* And whenever he shot an arrow at the target he also would *puffp!* He had five arrows... *puffp!* He shot them one at a time at the airborne target... *puffp! puffp! puffp! puffp!* He hit the target with all five arrows, and when he laughed with delight, he went *puffp!*

While Farting Boy was demonstrating his fine marksmanship, the wolves crept one at a time back into the camp, suspiciously sniffing the air. Coyote, who was out for his nightly prowl, came with the wolves. Coyote was a very smart fellow with a handsome coat and bright eyes.

"Hello, everybody, I am Coyote," he told Anpao and Farting Boy. "Perhaps you have heard of me. I'm very famous. Everyone always talks about Coyote and how smart and handsome he is. That's me . . . Coyote. I'm the very one that everybody always talks about. Perhaps you've heard about me."

"No," said Anpao. "I have never heard of you."

"Well," Coyote said glibly, smiling, "that's because you are probably a fool." Before Anpao could object, Coyote continued, "But if there were not fools, there could be no wise people. Since I am one of the wise ones, I shall help you to be less of a fool."

"But . . ." Anpao began.

Puffp! went the boy.

"What is that you have on your face?" Coyote asked Anpao. "What *is* that thing on your face? I have never seen anything like that."

"It is a scar," Anpao explained politely.

"Well, I think I would like to have that scar. How much do you want for it?"

"I can't give my scar away," Anpao told him. "I am keeping it for the Sun in the hope that he will remove it. In that way Ko-ko-mik-e-is will know that he has given us permission to be together."

"Nonsense," Coyote barked. "You don't need that scar, and besides I want it. Why don't you prove that you are not a fool and give it to me?"

Anpao laughed. "I'm sorry to laugh at you, but that's very foolish. How does it prove that I'm not a fool if I give you something I do not want to give you?"

"That's very simple," Coyote said. "If you weren't a fool you would understand exactly what I mean. But since you are a fool, it is senseless to try to explain anything to you. So that is why you should give me that scar."

Anpao laughed again. "But you are talking in circles and you didn't answer my question."

"That is more nonsense," Coyote said, with a polite smile. "Nobody can talk in circles. You can run in circles and you can draw circles, but you cannot talk in circles. If you don't understand that it is impossible to talk in circles, how can I possibly explain why you should give me your scar? You are clearly asking the impossible and, though I am very clever, I must admit to you that I cannot do the impossible except when I have the time."

The boy giggled. *Puffp-puffp-puffp!*

"What did you say?" Coyote asked him.

"Oh," explained Anpao, "this is my new friend Farting Boy and he didn't say anything."

"Hmmm," said Coyote. "Well, your thing certainly makes a marvelous noise. What do you call that thing?"

"Ha!" exclaimed Anpao gleefully. "Since you are so very wise, certainly you know the name of that thing."

Puffp!

"Hey, Farting Boy," Coyote said very nicely. "Don't pay any attention to your friend. Listen to me. I'm a very nice fellow and I would truly like to have that noise-making thing of yours."

"No," said Farting Boy. "It's mine and I want to keep it." And as he moved away from Coyote the thing went *puffp!*

"Aw, please, let me have it," Coyote pleaded.

"Well..." Farting Boy considered the situation for a moment. "All right," he said. "You can have it. All that noise only tires me out anyway. So you can have the bow, the arrows, the target, and all of the rest of it."

Coyote was overjoyed. He took his new possessions and strutted around proudly. "Tell me something," he said. "How do I throw the target?"

"It's easy. Let me show you." So Farting Boy showed Coyote how to throw the target and how to shoot the arrows.

Coyote threw it. *Puffp!*

And Coyote shot an arrow at it. *Puffp!* All five arrows. *Puffp! Puffp! Puffp! Puffp!*

"Well," the boy said happily. "I must leave now. Goodby!" And he ran off as fast as he could go.

That's when the trouble began. Every time Coyote moved, the thing would go *puffp!* Even when he tried to walk very slowly, *puffppppppp!* Even when he took tiny little steps, *pu-pu-pu-puff!* And when he carefully crept along, *puuuuuuuuuuuuuuuffp!* It wouldn't stop for a minute. It wasn't long before his thing got sore.

"Oh!" Coyote cried to Anpao. "You have to find that

boy and get him to take this terrible thing back! It feels like it is about to explode!" *P-U-F-F-P! ! !*

So Anpao hurried off as fast as he could to try to find the boy and urge him to take his thing back. Coyote was absolutely frantic by this time and chased around wildly. *PUFFP! PUFFP! PUFFPPP!*

"Where are you, boy? I want to give you back all your things!"

Though Coyote shouted and Anpao shouted, the boy didn't answer. By this time Coyote was feeling very remorseful about his thing. He sat still and didn't even move a muscle . . . but every time he took a breath . . . *puffffffp!*

"Oh!" cried Coyote, stamping his foot in a rage and racing around the campfire. "Somebody must do something at once!"

PUFFP! PUFFP! PUFFP! PUFFP! PUFFP! PUFFP! PUFFP! PUFFP! PUFFP!

"But this is nonsense." Anpao laughed as he watched Coyote race around the fire. "You seem to be talking in circles again!"

"Oh, please, please, please," Coyote begged in tears, "tell me, tell me, tell me! What can I do and how can I get rid of this thing? It hurts something terrible! I might even die and that would be the end of Coyote for sure!"

"But you are such a clever fellow," Anpao said, with a grin. "Surely you can figure it out for yourself. No matter what I tell you, you will only say that that's the one thing you forgot."

"Aw! Aw! Aw!" shouted Coyote as he ran faster and

faster, holding his thing and shouting as loud as he could shout. Finally in desperation he raced to the river and sat in the water to soothe the soreness... *pugpugpugpugpugggg*.

"Maybe if you were not so envious and if you gave up the bow and arrows and the target, perhaps that would help," Anpao finally told him, feeling sorry for Coyote and hoping he had learned his lesson.

"Ah," said Coyote as he threw down the things he had taken from Farting Boy. He felt better at once. "That is the one thing I forgot. That just goes to prove how really clever I am. Because if I was not wise enough to ask, you would never have been smart enough to tell me what to do! Now, how about that scar of yours..."

"Oh!" Anpao exclaimed and ran away from Coyote as fast as he could.

Deer Woman

◆

Wherever Anpao went, the men of the tribes honored him. They would urge him to marry one of their daughters and settle among their people. They greatly respected Anpao for his wisdom and they competed for the honor of feasting him when he stayed with them. Then, after the feast, they would coax Anpao to tell the marvelous tale of his long journey.

Anpao would recount his adventures and would thank his hosts graciously, but he was always anxious to continue on his way. He would explain to his new friends that he could not marry and settle down until he had found the lodge of the Sun and fulfilled his promise to Ko-ko-mik-e-is.

"But you must not leave us today, Anpao," urged the chief of a village where Anpao had lingered for many days. "Tonight we celebrate our great victory with a Scalp Dance. You must not miss it, my friend, for many of our most beautiful girls wish to honor you. So stay with us at least until after our celebration!"

Anpao agreed, and that night the great celebration brought many handsomely dressed people from villages near and far. An immense fire was built and the men and women rejoiced in the roaring light of the flames. The victory songs sailed over the plain. Girls danced in a circle around the fire, carrying scalps on long poles to show the bravery of their brothers, who had counted many coups in battle and taken many scalps. The young women joined hands and delicately stepped in a circle, while the young men, in their feathered bustles and with precious strands of fur braided into their thick black hair, each danced alone inside the ring formed by the girls.

While the people danced and the great fire sent dazzling flames high into the sky and spread wild, leaping shadows across the grass, a strange woman appeared out of the darkness and slipped unnoticed between two girls in the circle, and began to dance with the others.

This woman was extremely beautiful—so beautiful that Anpao could not keep his eyes off of her. When he smiled at the stranger, all the girls who had hoped to win his attentions noticed her and became sullen.

"Do you see how he looks at her?" the girls complained. "Now there is no chance for any of us!"

If the girls had looked down at the woman's feet, they would have quickly understood her exceptional attraction and power, for this beautiful stranger did not have the feet of a woman but the hoofs of a deer, and no moccasins could possibly conceal them. But unfortunately the girls did not notice. Nor did the young men, for they could see nothing but the woman's astonishing beauty and her luminous eyes.

All evening Anpao had not stopped gazing at the black eyes of Deer Woman. But she paid no attention to him. She looked at all the other young men and finally selected a strong handsome boy who was sitting with his pretty girl friend. The boy had paid no attention to Deer Woman, but when she fixed her glistening eyes on him he was helpless. Suddenly, all he could think about was the supple body of the woman who stood alone, gazing at him from the far side of the fire. He could no longer stay with his girl friend, even though he loved her dearly. Instead, he slowly stood up and then abruptly left the girl. She called after him but he took no notice. Deer Woman smiled at him with her magic eyes and, as the Moon was sinking out of the dark sky, she drew him away with her into the bushes.

When Deer Woman vanished with the young man, Anpao had a sense of release. Instead of being jealous, he felt relieved because the burning in his body that had been ignited by her gaze had ceased. But the girl friend of the boy who had gone off with Deer Woman was not relieved. Anpao tried to comfort her, but nothing could help her sorrow. She wept bitterly and would listen to nothing Anpao told her. He promised that he would find her lover as soon as the Sun rose and would persuade him to leave the strange woman. But still the girl cried and Anpao could do nothing more to help her till morning.

As Anpao left the grieving girl, he felt so weary that he could barely reach his sleeping place. No sooner had he put his head to the earth than a great sleep filled with the eyes of the strange woman rolled over him.

In the morning the camp was covered by a dismal mist and all the joy of the previous night was gone. Anpao was awakened by someone running through the encampment shouting hysterically. When the people had calmed the frightened boy, he gasped as he told them in a terrified voice that he had found the young man who had gone off with the strange woman.

"It is terrible!" he gasped again and again. "It is terrible! You must not let his girl friend see it!" he muttered in horror. "I stumbled upon him in the bushes. He was lying on his back, stripped and naked, in the place where they had made love. No, no, I cannot tell you how he died! I cannot speak of it!" The boy groaned and ran into his lodge where he could be alone.

Anpao quickly gathered his bow and arrows and ran into the bushes. Almost at once he came upon the dead youth. He looked away with utter horror. "Ah!" he groaned. "Who has done this terrible thing to you, my poor friend?"

The old women crept up beside Anpao and began to wail as they knelt by the dead boy. "*Ayi...* it was that one! It was *she!*" an ancient woman whispered, with terror in her old eyes. "It was *she* who did this—Deer Woman!"

"That strange woman in the dance ring..." another woman whispered as she wept and laid her cheek on the boy's bruised shoulder. "We should have known it was she! We should have known by the way she stood and by the way she looked at all our handsome young men! Ah, we should have known it!" And the wrinkled old woman wept.

"But *look*... just look at him!" Anpao gasped, covering his face. "How did she do such a thing to him?"

"Ah," the woman moaned, as she embraced the boy and nodded her head in a daze, rocking back and forth as she droned. "That is the way it is with Deer Woman. She holds the young men with those magic eyes of hers. She lures them into the darkness with her beauty. And then, after she has taken her pleasure with them, while they are still lying contentedly in the grass suspecting nothing, then suddenly she hits them. Yes, she is so strong . . . I cannot tell you how strong she is! And she struck this poor boy, fiercely, fiercely. And while he was recovering from the brutal attack and was trying to get up, Deer Woman laughed at him and leaped over him, pushing him to the ground where she trampled and trampled his groin with her knife-edged hoofs! That is what she does—she tramples the groin of her lover in a furious victory dance which does not end until he shudders and bleeds and dies."

For a moment there was silence except for the weeping. Then the old woman whispered in a dry voice, "Then Deer Woman is gone. She slips away, her legs splattered with blood, leaving a crimson trail like the tracks of a doe."

Anpao sat silently in the forest while the old women lovingly cleaned and wrapped the body of the young man and prepared his burial platform. Anpao could hear nothing but the mourning song of the girl who had loved the boy, the stifled screams of the boy's mother.

When night came again, Anpao was afraid to stay alone in the forest. He hurried back into the village, where he collected his possessions, determined to leave this sad place as soon as the Sun appeared in the sky. He was frightened of the night and could not sleep. But he was afraid to stray from other people. He hurried through the darkness that hovered between the little fires in front of the widely separated lodges. He was exhausted but still he could not sleep while the face of Deer Woman lingered in his mind. He did not want to be alone. More than anything else, he feared being alone. So when he saw a man sitting in front of his solitary lodge, one of the few people still awake, he hurried to him and asked if he could share his fire.

"You are welcome, my boy. I am very old, as you can see, and I always need a warm fire because the life in me has turned into a long, long winter, which will not see spring again. I am so old that the Sun shuns me as if I were already gone. That is why I cannot sleep. I have a horror of sleep and I try to avoid it. You see, my son, I have to stay awake as much as I can, otherwise the animals might think that I am already dead and carry me off before I am ready." Then the ancient eyes returned to the fire and he was silent.

"I am grateful, old father, that you have let me sit with you," Anpao said quietly, looking into the face of this incredibly old person who sat hunched on the ground in the glow of the fire, with the sagging breasts of a woman and withered tendrils of flesh hanging from his collapsed skeleton.

For a long time the two men sat silently huddled over the only fire still burning in the otherwise pitch-dark camp. The old one wheezed steadily, nodding his head and blankly staring off into the darkness, as if he sensed something or someone. The gaze of those gray, dim eyes frightened Anpao and he darted a glance behind to see what the man was looking at. There was an immense wall of darkness and nothing more.

"Yes," the ancient one murmured as he very gradually turned his glassy eyes to stare through Anpao. "That was Deer Woman. All I have ever seen of her is the back of her head. I am too old. She cares nothing for old men. But young men ... she likes the young ones. She comes and she goes and we can do nothing to stop her. No one knows who she is or where she comes from. No one knows for certain how or where she lives when she is not dancing. She is always appearing and disappearing and no one knows where she might be seen next. Late at night, when the Stomp Dance lines twist around the fire, Deer Woman vanishes.

"Sometimes she takes a young man with her and sometimes a young woman. The girls are usually found the next day, lying in the woods, beaten and bloody. If they are still alive, they are crippled for life. They are ugly. Sometimes the girls vanish and are never seen again. Deer Woman controls those girls and keeps them hidden somewhere. Perhaps they also become Deer Women—who knows?

"All the men of the villages, they try to keep a watch for Deer Woman. They want to protect the boys and girls from her, but she has great power. As soon as a beautiful strange woman appears, instead of guessing that it might be Deer Woman, the young men fall under the power of her eyes and forget the danger. So no one has ever caught her. She comes and she goes. She comes and she goes.

"Only once the men kept a careful watch for her— many years ago when I was a young man. They all kept their eyes on the ground and would not look up at any woman's face, no matter how beautiful she might be. That was clever of those men because they could not be caught by the power of Deer Woman's eyes. They could only see her feet. That's what happened! A woman came along and they saw that her feet were not feet but hoofs! One of the strongest men pounced on her and almost grabbed her, but that Deer Woman, she's strong, and she jumped straight up in the air maybe ten feet high, and off she ran into the night in great leaps so high and so fast that no person could catch up with her!"

All Anpao could do was shake his head in amazement. "Horrible," he whispered. "I am strong and I am not afraid of many things, but I have never seen anything as terrible as the way that boy was killed. Of all the things I have had to face on my long journey this is the worst."

"This thing that terrifies you, my son, it is called Death." The old man shrugged. "The young know nothing of it. They think that life goes on and on until one day you lie down peacefully and go to sleep. But Death is not like that. It is something no one wants but everyone receives. It is like Deer Woman. Though you fear her you cannot resist her. Some say that it is better if we never see her. But there are also people who believe she is so beautiful that it is worth dying for her. That is what they say."

"I don't want to think about it," Anpao said, walking slowly away from the old man.

"You need not think about it, my young friend; it will think about you. It will happen whether you think about it or not. When I look across the river and beyond the valleys, when I search for the faces of my friends who are gone, I cannot help thinking about the day when everything must die and all that has been can be no more. I sometimes sit here under a storm of stars watching them burn their desperate, separate fires in the enormous sky. But always as I watch something happens. Look... you will see it too. There— a star dies! It makes a great flash of fire as it falls. And then it dies. There is not a night when some great star does not fall. One day even our father the Sun will fall. All the stars are fathers and all must die. I do not understand it, my son. I do not try. I know only that there is a thing called Death and we cannot understand how good it is to be alive until we have seen the stars, the birds, our fathers fall."

Anpao hurried away. He didn't want to hear any more. Then for just a moment he paused and looked back at the ancient man who sat in the glow of his small fire in the cavernous darkness of the world. "It is a wonder," he called out to the man, "that you want to stay alive if you feel like that. Nothing makes any sense if everything has to end."

For an instant the old man smiled rather sadly. Then he nodded slowly and said, "No, my son, the wonder is that it has happened at all."

The Drowned Boys

Again it was summer. The ground groaned for water and the trees recoiled from the ferocious glare of the Sun, whose dazzling face burned a great wound in the sky, thrashing the clouds into dust and turning the heavens' blue to white.

Though Anpao had been living among the people of the Cross Timbers for a very long time, he was still a stranger among them. He had no one to make moccasins for him and no one to make him clothes. Only the old women pitied him and gave him food. The young men admired Anpao and sometimes they provided him with shelter and old clothing. But being unmarried and an outsider left Anpao an alien wherever he went.

"You are a good hunter," one of Anpao's young friends told him. "If you will take my brother and me to the hunting grounds beyond our lands and show us the buffaloes you told us about, we will give you a new pair of moccasins and enough food and supplies to help you over the mountains where you can continue your search for the Sun."

"It is too hot and I don't want to be responsible for you and your brother. What if something happens to you? Then what will I tell your people?"

"We will give you three pairs of moccasins and all the food you can carry! Please, you must show us these buffaloes!"

"I have no interest in making a journey. If I did, I would be searching for the Sun instead of spending all my days here," Anpao said sullenly.

"Then why do you stay any longer? If you will be our scout and show us the way, we will supply you with everything you need to continue your journey. And when we have reached the hunting grounds beyond our land, you may go on without us and we will return here on our own. Think of it, Anpao! You could not find a better offer. That will bring you much closer to your journey's end. Tell me, Anpao, will you do it if we give you new leggings and many pairs of moccasins and food for your journey?"

"I cannot refuse such an offer," Anpao said with a smile. "I will do it, but only if we travel in the direction of the setting Sun, for it is only there that I wish to go."

"Good!" the youth exclaimed with excitement, for he had never been very far from the edge of the Cross Timbers where he was born. "Then it is agreed!"

The young men quickly made their plans, collecting their stone-headed axes and their spears. They gathered food and packed it carefully in rawhide sacks. They hung many extra moccasins around their necks. Then after much preparation, they gathered the bundles of provisions which their families had prepared for them and started out on foot toward the setting Sun.

Anpao glanced up at the blazing Sun but it gave him

no welcome. So much time had passed since the Sun and Anpao had known each other in the World-Above-the-World that the father no longer recognized his son.

After many days of walking, the young men came to the low ridges that bordered their homeland. Beyond the ridges, the landscape was very flat and more barren than any place the young men had ever seen.

"You must remember," Anpao told his friends, "when you make the trip back to your village, to be sure to follow these posts of yucca that you see. This place is called the Staked Plains, because the people who live here mark the trails from one water hole to the next with yucca stubs. Without this trail you would soon die of thirst."

As they stumbled across the desolation, the boys soon saw the truth of Anpao's caution. Here and there, half buried in the drifts of gray sand, were the bones of men who had lost their way. Lizards and ants nestled in the shade of the skulls and great ants scampered in and out of sockets and joints.

"Why does anyone want to live in such a barren place?" the boys asked. Everywhere they looked there was the burned, gray plain shimmering into the distance in tidal waves of heat and dust. There was not a bird in the sky, but only undulating rolls of heat rising from the endless horizon of white light.

After following the yucca stakes for a long distance, the hunting party came to a place where the ground abruptly tumbled away at their feet, falling straight down into a deep, narrow canyon of sand and rock. They could not descend, for the ground was too soft, and as they continued along the brink their ears were filled with the receding rumble of landslides as rock and sand tumbled into the chasm.

In the blasts of heat that bristled from the earth the boys could see something far, far out in the flatlands—something shining, like water spreading out into a wide lake. But when they got to the place where they had seen the lake, there was nothing there. Nothing but more sand. Then suddenly one of the brothers cried out in delight. "It's a rabbit!" he shouted, raising his bow and shooting into the blinding clouds of dust. But when he ran to pick it up, it had disappeared. Not even a bloodstain remained. The boy returned to his friends with an uneasy look on his face. Just when he was about to speak, he heard the noise of a crowd of people behind him. They were angry and they shouted as they ran forward. The boys did not dare look behind to find out what was happening but ran headlong into the dust. The angry voices followed in their tracks and came close behind them. Then Anpao knew that they would be overtaken and would have to fight. He wheeled around and looked back.

There was no one in sight, only the rolls of heat and the sand.

"Why were we running?" one of the boys asked in confusion, as he slumped to the ground and tried to catch his breath.

"But it was you who started running!" Anpao barked at him.

"No, it was my brother. I'm certain it was he!"

"No, it was not I! That's a lie! I ran because you started to run!"

As the young men began to quarrel, Anpao tried to calm them down and begged them not to run away from things that didn't exist. He also had a difficult time preventing the brothers from dashing out into the burning landscape to splash into lakes that weren't there.

"Ah!" shouted one of them, when they had resumed their journey along the trail of yucca stakes. "Look, Anpao, please take a look! It is real, I swear to you, it is real this time!"

Anpao ignored the boy's words until his brother also began to shout that he too saw something in the distance. When Anpao followed their frantic gestures and peered into the dust, shading his eyes with his hand, he thought he saw something, something shining, on the ground . . . something shining with a silvery light far ahead of them.

"No, no," Anpao muttered with annoyance. "You are being children. There is nothing there. You must think about something else or you will surely go mad. You must stop thinking about water!"

So the disgruntled hunting party continued sullenly along the trail of yucca posts. As they laboriously made their way through the soft sand, the thing shining in the distance grew larger and larger. Soon the brothers began to hurry toward it despite the terrible heat. Anpao shouted to them to conserve their energy, but they wouldn't listen to him. "Do you see?" one brother exclaimed. "It is very large! It is like a great mound of ice, like a giant crystal of water. Anpao, look! It is like the Sun! It is like the Sun, Anpao!"

"Ah!" Anpao whispered. "Perhaps it is truly the Sun at last! Perhaps we have found the place where the Sun sleeps!"

It certainly could have been the Sun, for the great object in the distance glittered like a silver star. "Yes," Anpao shouted. "You are right! We must hurry! We must hurry before it is gone!"

And the young men began to run in the awful blaze of the Sun's heat until their bodies were covered with sweat and their breath was gone and they could run no farther. They fell to the ground and groaned with exhaustion. Then, after they had rested briefly, they continued with great effort along the trail. As they trudged through the dust, they tried to moisten their cracked lips and they wiped the sand from their eyes and peered into the distance where the great silver crystal glistened and glowed. They followed the trail for many hours, hoping at any moment to reach the Sun—but as they hurried and staggered and stumbled toward the emanation in the flatlands, the Sun moved farther and farther away, until at last it stood high in the sky and seared their bodies with its roar.

"Wait," Anpao groaned. "Do you see what has happened? That thing ahead of us cannot be the Sun, for the Sun is now above us, while the silver mound has not moved from its place in the West. Ah, it is not the Sun after all." He sank dejectedly to the baked ground, while the others, taking no notice of his words, staggered on ahead of him. Anpao put his head on the burning sand and closed his eyes. He did not care any longer. He could not continue on such a cruel journey. Perhaps the people who urged him to get married and settle down were right after all. Perhaps there was no Ko-ko-mik-e-is—perhaps, like the lakes which appeared and disappeared in the desert, she was only a mirage created by his thirst for a home. Perhaps it was all an illusion and a terrible ordeal which signified nothing.

After he had lain in the scorching heat for a long while, he heard the faint voices of the brothers calling to him in the distance. "Anpao! Anpao! Come, please come and see this mystery we have found! Anpao!"

He had no power left in his body, for he felt certain that he would never find his father the Sun and would never be able to return to Ko-ko-mik-e-is. This desert was surely the end of the world, but there was still no end in sight. There was nowhere left to go. It was too late. Anpao was already at an age when he should be a man, and yet he had not received his father's blessing. And now it was too late.

"Anpao! Anpao! Please, come quickly and see this marvelous thing we have discovered!" The distant voices came to him over the sand.

Slowly Anpao got up and started walking again, moving toward the voices of the brothers without looking up.

When he finally caught up with the others, he looked up despondently and was amazed at what he saw. Towering over the flatlands was a creature—a gigantic turtle with a shell like a many-faceted crystal that was so silvery and bright that it shone like the Sun. The brothers were running excitedly beside the creature and shouting at it, but it ignored them and continued along its way, moving very slowly, one leg at a time, following the yucca stakes.

"Ha!" shouted one of the brothers. "Watch me! I'm

going to take a ride on the monster's back!" And he quickly leaped onto the rim of the turtle's silver shell and scampered to the top. The creature paid no attention. It continued to crawl along the trail without looking to the left or to the right, and it ignored the shouts of the foolish brother.

"Anpao! Why don't you come up here too? He's a very strong creature and can carry all of us!"

"No!" Anpao said. "You should get down and leave this mystery alone. You are making fun of him and it will come to no good for you."

But the young man ignored Anpao. He called to his brother and coaxed him to leap onto the turtle's back. The young fellow made several efforts to reach the creature's back before he finally succeeded. Now only Anpao was left on the ground, walking beside the great creature and shouting to his frivolous friends. "Get down!" he ordered in anger. "We can walk along with him and keep him company, but he is too powerful to be treated so badly. Come down right away!"

The boys on the turtle's back laughed at Anpao. "You are always worrying. You never have any fun, Anpao; that's your problem. You are supposed to be a great hunter and warrior, but I think perhaps you are a coward! All you know is Ko-ko-mik-e-is!" High on the giant turtle's back, they jumped up and down on the huge crystalline shell. But the turtle paid no attention to them. They laughed and taunted Anpao; they pranced around and pried at the facets of the turtle's shell with their spears, but the turtle only continued to walk slowly along the trail of yucca posts.

"Stop it!" Anpao shouted in a rage. "You are behaving like fools! How foolish you are to think that so great a being was created just to amuse you! Get down right away or I warn you something terrible will happen to you!"

Just as Anpao spoke, a cloud abruptly came into the clear sky and passed in front of the Sun, turning the desert dark. A cold wind swept through the blistering atmosphere, chilling the young men and making them tremble. Suddenly they searched the landscape in fear, feeling something awful coming down upon them. The younger brother cried out and started to scramble off the turtle's back.

"You are right, Anpao," he whimpered, as he edged toward the ground. "Something terrible is going to happen!"

But when the boy tried to leap from the rim of the turtle's shell he discovered to his horror that his moccasins had turned to silver and the soles were melted fast to the crystalline creature's back.

"Ah! Anpao, help me! Please! I cannot come down!" he screamed in a terrified voice.

Then the older brother also tried to climb down. But his moccasins began to glow with a ferocious heat and he could not move his feet. The older brother began to attack the turtle with his ax and spear. He struck it on the head and tried to beat the animal to make it stop. But his weapons only shattered against the gigantic turtle, which continued along slowly without looking to the right or to the left.

Then the young men wept and cried out to Anpao, "Please, try to help us! You are the oldest and you promised to protect us if we gave you food and supplies. You have to do something to help us, Anpao!"

Anpao ran to the head of the turtle and looked at it in desperation. "Please, my ancient friend," he begged, "please forgive my friends and let them get down. We won't bother you ever again, I promise. We will stay here until you have gone away in peace and we won't ever do such an evil thing again! Please, my powerful friend, be merciful and forgive these foolish brothers; they are very young and do not know that they must show respect for everything that is in the world! Please let them go free and they will honor you forever!"

But the great turtle continued on its way, crawling very slowly, one leg at a time, and the young men could not get down from its glittering back.

Anpao ran beside the turtle weeping as he listened to the piteous voices of his friends, but the turtle crawled on and on, and the young men could not get down.

The clouds continued to rise in the sky, making it so gloomy and so cold that Anpao shivered as he hurried after the turtle. The desert, which moments before had radiated with the glow of a thousand fires, was now forlorn and dark. The day was ending, but still the great turtle crawled on.

"Ah, no!" Anpao groaned, for just ahead he could see a large water hole—a pool of dead water which bubbled and stank and lay dead and purple in a hollow of the flatlands. "Oh!" Anpao wept, for now he knew it was toward that pool of dead water that the turtle was relentlessly crawling.

At that same moment the young men fastened to the turtle's back also saw the water, and they screamed in fear. They began to cry for mercy and they began to pray to the turtle, but it ignored them and continued to crawl along on its way, slowly moving toward the pool of purple mire where the trail of yucca posts ended.

"Stop! Stop!" shouted Anpao. "Please stop and let my friends go. Show us your great strength through your mercy!"

But the turtle still crawled toward the terrible water.

Then Anpao faltered and looked up at the young men who frantically beat at the shell of the turtle and sobbed and screamed in horrid voices.

"What can I do to help you?" Anpao exclaimed.

But they did not hear him. They fell down and screamed and wailed. When their arms touched the turtle's glistening shell, they stuck fast and glowed with a fantastic heat. When they fell down their bodies glistened like white coals, and they shrieked in pain and pleaded for help. Anpao could do nothing but watch them die.

"Go away!" the younger brother whimpered to him. "Quickly, quickly, get away and save yourself, Anpao! There is nothing you can do for us now—we are lost. Run away and find your father before you too are destroyed!"

But Anpao could not leave them. He chased after the turtle even when the sand became soft under his feet and he began to sink into the ground. He shouted and yelled and struggled forward through the quicksand, hardly able to move his feet in the soft mire that sucked him down.

"Go away!" yelled the young brother, who was slowly turning white and then gray and then silver.

"Oh," Anpao moaned as he backed away to escape the quicksand. "My poor friends . . ." He raised his arms and waved frantically, trying to give them courage.

The young brother gasped for breath and feebly raised his arm as the gigantic creature stepped into the murky water. Anpao shuddered as the animal carried the boys gradually down and down into the putrescent water and the young brother weakly waved his arm and wept. Anpao watched as the turtle slowly submerged into the ooze and only the heads of the two boys were still visible. And then the bubbles poured from their mouths and noses, and their eyes filled with an incredible horror, and they were gone.

There was nothing left now. Only darkness. Then the black clouds slithered back across the pallid sky, and the Moon slowly turned her head toward Anpao and smiled.

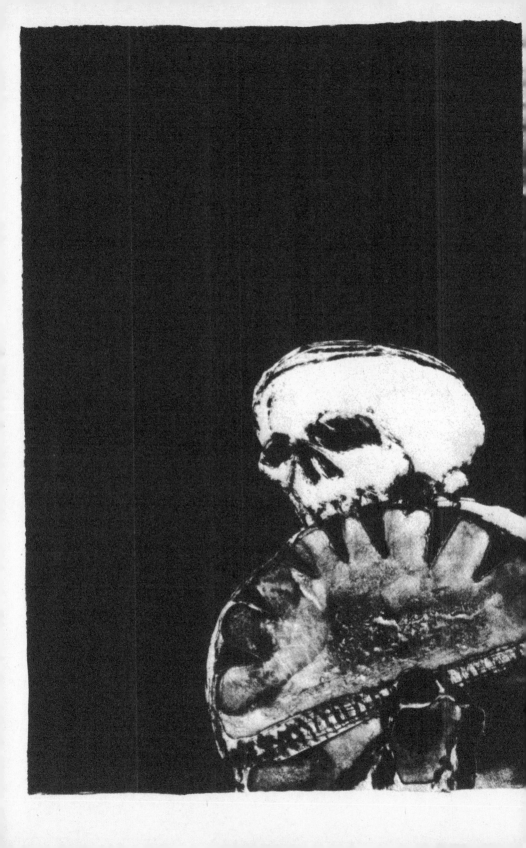

IV

The Invasion from the Sea

The Sun Journey

A̲t last Anpao had reached the edge of the vast desert where
the light of the Sun was so strong that only the hum-
blest creatures and plants could survive among the crags and
drifts of sand. He stood on a narrow ribbon of earth from
which the slopes of a wide valley plunged without pause.
A thousand feet straight down, the striated yellow, buff, and
rose flanks of the canyon were textured by small herds of
black pines. Behind him, on the brink of this enormous
earthwork, a lonely hawk flew ceaselessly in a desolate gray
sky. Surely this was the edge of the world and the place
where Anpao's father, the Sun, lived.

He started carefully down the trail, knowing that at any
moment something unexpected might happen . . . knowing
that nothing was exactly what it seemed to be.

Then Anpao stopped and stared at the ground. On the
trail lay the most beautiful objects he had ever seen. There
was a war shirt, a shield, and a bow and arrows. Anpao had
never seen such handsome weapons. And he had never seen
such a noble war shirt. His own clothes had become shabby
from the long journey in the desert. His last pair of moccasins
was torn and his hair was knotted and filthy. He crouched so
he could gaze at the beautiful things on the ground. It seemed

as if someone had surely left them there so any passerby could take them. But Anpao would not touch them. He got up and walked carefully around the objects and continued on his way.

"*Kyi*," came a voice.

Anpao spun around in fear.

"Don't be afraid. I intend you no harm." It was a young man, standing just off the trail and smiling a very friendly smile, such as Anpao had not seen since he left the village of Ko-ko-mik-e-is. He was the handsomest person Anpao had ever seen. His hair was long and he wore clothes made of marvelous, strange skins. His moccasins were sewn with bright-colored feathers and his necklaces were made of bits of stone that shone like sunlight.

"Tell me the truth," the young man said to Anpao. "Did you see some weapons on the trail?"

"Yes, I saw them," Anpao said.

The young man looked at him with curiosity for a moment. Then he asked, "And you didn't take them?"

"No," Anpao said. "I am a stranger here and the weapons did not belong to me. So I did not take them."

"You are a person, are you not?"

"Yes, I am a person—I'm certain of it."

The young man laughed. "And yet you did not steal those beautiful weapons? Is it possible that there is a person from the world who is not a thief?" Anpao looked at the young man blankly. "What is your name?" the handsome youth asked.

"Anpao."

"Why have you come across the terrible desert and where do you think you are going?"

"I wish to find the Sun."

"Ah, then you have come to the right place," the young man said, smiling. "My name is A-pi-su-ahts... Morning Star. The Sun is my father."

"But that's impossible!" Anpao said, and laughed.

Morning Star looked annoyed; he was not accustomed to being contradicted or laughed at. "What do you mean, *impossible?*"

Anpao was about to explain that he himself was the son of the Sun, but he reconsidered. After all, Morning Star looked like the son of a very great person, whereas Anpao looked so wretched that no one would believe that he was a son of the mighty Sun. And for all Anpao knew, the Sun might not even recognize him any longer. It had been so long since he had last seen his father. So rather than endanger himself, Anpao kept his secret.

"Oh," he said calmly, "I simply meant that I could hardly believe that I have finally found the real home of the great Sun. For if the Sun is your father—and I do not doubt it for a minute—then this surely must be the place where the Sun lives ... and my journey is finished at last!"

"Well," Morning Star said conceitedly, "I am indeed the son of the Sun, and since you are not a thief I will take you to our lodge. You are rather dirty, but I have no one here who is my own age. I guess you are better company than no company at all."

Anpao brushed the dust from his arms and shoulders

self-consciously and felt very humble in comparison to the elegant and grand Morning Star. He waited for the young man to show him the way and then he followed at a distance, trying to imitate the graceful manners of this dandified son of the Sun. But every time Anpao came too close, Morning Star would stop with disdain and make a face and sniff the air as if he smelled something foul. He shook his head in dismay and huffed, "Well, at least you are not a thief—that's one thing I can say in your favor."

Soon they came in sight of a marvelous and very lavish lodge, which was cradled in a beautiful little valley where trees and flowered vines shone with a silvery light. "My father is not at home," Morning Star said elegantly, "but he will come back tonight. Brush yourself off and then you may come in."

The lodge was large and extremely handsome. Strange medicine-animals were painted everywhere. Behind the lodge, on a tripod of elaborately carved posts, the Sun's fantastic clothes and his spectacular weapons were carefully hung.

"Come in, come in," urged Morning Star impatiently. "Don't just stand there—come in before I change my mind and send you back to the desert!" But Anpao was ashamed to enter the beautiful lodge in his shabby clothes. He was also frightened, for the mother of Morning Star might not be a generous woman. "Come along, come along," said Morning Star. "Don't be afraid. I am glad you have come. I have always been very lonely and, if you will behave yourself and take a bath, you can be my friend."

Anpao took a deep breath. He realized that he had to

be brave if he was to speak to the Sun and get permission to have Ko-ko-mik-e-is as his wife. So he stepped into the lodge with an assurance which would have pleased Grandmother Spider.

There was only one person sitting inside—the Sun's wife and Morning Star's mother. It was the Moon.

Anpao's heart stopped and he turned to run away, but the Moon said, "Please, my boy, come in and welcome."

Anpao blinked his eyes and gazed with disbelief at the terrible white face of the Moon. "Please sit down and eat something, for surely you are hungry after your journey across the vast desert land," she said in a kind voice. "Who are you, my boy, and why have you come so far from your own people?"

Anpao stared at her and could not move. Was it possible that the Moon did not recognize him after having chased and haunted him his entire life? Was it a trick, or was it possible that he had changed so much in becoming a young man that his great and fearsome enemy no longer knew his face?

Peering with fear at the Moon, Anpao edged forward carefully and sat down very slowly. He winced when she reached toward him and opened her hand. In it was something to eat. He sighed with relief and tried to command as much courage as he could in the presence of this formidable enemy.

"But, young man, you have not answered my questions," the Moon said gently. "You are welcome here and have no need to be afraid. Tell us your name and why you have come."

"He told me," Morning Star began, "that his name . . ."
But before he could say more, Anpao interrupted him.

"My name is Scarface," he blurted out quickly, fearful
that the Moon would recognize the name Anpao.

"But," objected Morning Star, "I thought you told me
that your name . . ."

"Ah," interrupted Anpao nervously, "forget whatever
I told you. I didn't want to tell you my real name. After all,
who wants to be called Scarface all his life? It's a terrible
name and I hate it!"

"I do not blame you at all for disliking your name,"
the Moon said. "It is a pity for a young man to have such
a mark upon his face. How did you come by it?"

"It is because of this scar that I have come," Anpao
explained, carefully calculating his words. "I have come to
ask the great Sun to remove this scar from my face."

"Ah, well, it is true of course that the Sun is very
powerful, as we all know. And he can do many great things.
But I am not certain that he will want to remove your scar,"
the Moon told Anpao as she prepared dinner for the Sun.
"He is not very fond of people, for one thing, and for another, he may be a bit angry that you have crossed the desert
and come to our home."

"I mean no disrespect and I have come such a long
way . . ."

"Yes, you have surely come a long way," the Moon
agreed. "And the Sun will certainly commend you for your
courage and daring, but you must understand that the Sun
doesn't like people. Once he was foolish and while I was

away at night he took a woman as his mistress. She was just like all people—very evil and selfish. Eventually the Sun had to kill her. I forgave him for his foolishness, but he has never forgiven the woman who tried to run back to the world of people. No, the Sun does not like people."

"But didn't the Sun have another child?" Anpao asked.

The Moon winced at the question and her eyes glowed horribly. The lodge trembled and Morning Star gasped in fear. "You must not ask questions!" he warned Anpao. "You will not be welcome here if you ever speak of such things again!"

"I am sorry," Anpao mumbled fearfully. "I did not mean to make you angry, great Moon. It is just that I have traveled a very long distance and everywhere I have gone I heard among the creatures about the Sun's other son . . ."

Again the lodge shook, and the Moon rose to her feet and made a horrendous sound, like an avalanche of ice shattering and plummeting into space. "He is dead!" she shrieked. "That woman and her bastard child died together and are gone forever!"

"Please, no more of this, Mother!" pleaded Morning Star. "I see my father coming. He will be unhappy if he sees you like this."

When the Moon heard that her husband was coming, she suddenly became gracious and gentle again. She smiled at Anpao as if she forgave him, but he knew that behind her pretty smile was the savage Moon. He knew this for certain —there is always the other face of the Moon, which no one can see.

"Come quickly, Scarface," the Moon told him. "Hide under these skins until we find out if the Sun is in a good mood and if he will welcome a person to our lodge. Hurry, hide under here!"

Anpao crawled under the pile of robes and lay there quietly. Then he peeked out so he might see his great father the Sun for the first time in many years. There was a thunderous roar and the doorway of the lodge filled with golden light. Then a very tall and handsome man dressed in dazzling clothes appeared. His noble head was surrounded by a great thick mane of gleaming golden feathers. He was a more fantastic being than Anpao had ever imagined his great father to be. Tears came to Anpao's eyes as he peered out from the pile of hides and rapturously gazed at the Sun.

No sooner had the Sun entered the lodge than he snorted and said in a deep resonant voice, "Ah! I smell a person!"

"Yes, father," confessed Morning Star, smiling to try to soothe the Sun. "It is a young man who has come to see you. I know he is an honest fellow and not like other people, because he found some of my possessions on the trail and yet he did not take a one of them."

"Uh, I have no patience with people," the Sun muttered as he sat down and peered around the lodge for the intruder. "Let's take a look at this young man-person who has come to see me. Where have you hidden him?"

Then Anpao came out from under the robes and stood without the least fear, for, having seen his great father, he was filled with such pride and glory that he knew he would never be afraid again. He looked into his father's eyes, uncertain if the Sun would recognize him, and hoping that if he did he would be willing to protect him from the rage of the Moon.

For a long time the Sun studied Anpao's face. "What is your name?" he asked very thoughtfully.

"They call me Scarface," Anpao said.

"Uh, Scarface—well, that may be so. For a moment I thought I knew you. But the boy I knew was much smaller and he did not have a scar on his face. The boy I knew was . . ."

"Enough!" scolded the Moon. "That is something you promised never to discuss!"

"Uh," mumbled the Sun, "so I did. Well, Scarface, I am glad you have come to my lodge. So sit down and do not be frightened of me. I am not a bad fellow once you get to know me. I want you to stay with us and be our guest. My son is a lonely boy; he has not a single friend. If you don't mind his vanity and his fancy ways, perhaps you will become his friend. He takes after his mother and has no love of adventure. However, you will find that he is a good lad," the Sun said in his gruff manner. "And I think you can learn to love him as your brother."

"I am very grateful for your hospitality and kindness . . ." Anpao began, but the Sun interrupted him before he could finish.

"Yes, yes . . . well, that's fine. But now I am hungry and tired and I want to be alone. So why don't you and Morning Star go out and get to know each other." With that the Sun dismissed the young men and sat down to his dinner.

The next day the Moon called Anpao. "Morning Star," she told him, "is too much like his father. He loves to hunt and to run around all day. I think you are a wise young man because you have traveled far and survived many ordeals. So I will trust in you. But I want you to listen carefully to what I am about to tell you. You may go with Morning Star wherever you please, but one thing you must never do. Never hunt near the big water! Do you understand me? That is the one thing I tell you, Scarface, and you must obey me if you value your life. Never hunt near the water and do not let Morning Star go there."

"But why can't we hunt near the water?" Anpao asked.

"Ah!" the Moon snorted in annoyance. "Why must these human creatures always ask so many questions!"

"It is difficult to do something," Anpao said humbly, "if you do not understand why you are doing it."

The Moon sighed impatiently and explained, "The water is the home of gigantic evil birds with long, sharp bills. They kill precious things. They have killed before and they will do it again if they get the chance. I have had many sons, but these birds have killed them all. Morning Star is the only child left. We have protected him all his life. Now he is the only child who has survived and grown into a young man. Do you see? You must help us protect him."

"I understand," Anpao said. "But tell me . . ."

"Ah," sighed the Moon, "what now?"

"Do these birds kill people too?"

"No," she said. "They only kill the children of the Sun. So you are in no danger from them."

"Ah," whispered Anpao with a worried look.

Anpao and the Magic Dogs

Anpao and Morning Star became fast friends. They hunted together and they told each other tales. Morning Star loved to listen to the stories of Anpao's long journey to find the Sun, for that noble young man had never ventured from his home and knew nothing of the world beyond. Anpao loved to listen to the tales that Morning Star told about their great father the Sun, who had dazzled the entire world with his great strength and virility. Often Anpao wanted to confess to Morning Star that they were truly brothers and that his real name was Anpao—the Dawn. But he feared that his brother would not keep his secret, and he was sure that the Moon would tear him apart if she ever discovered his true identity.

At first Anpao tried to draw the Moon into conversation about the woman who had been the mistress of the Sun, for he longed to know more of his mother. But the Moon always became so fierce at the very mention of the woman that Anpao soon realized there was no use in trying to persuade her that her hatred for the woman and her son was unfair. The Moon was so jealous that she could not tolerate the thought of any woman, let alone the one who had been the Sun's mistress.

Anpao gave up his efforts to talk to the Moon. He feared that he would never be accepted by his father and would never be able to return to the village of Ko-ko-mik-e-is. It seemed very unlikely that he could ever get permission from the Sun to marry her. And though the Sun seemed to like him, he was certain that his father would never remove the scar from his face unless he knew Anpao's true identity.

There was no hope at all for Anpao. He was in terrible danger of losing his life to the Moon if he told his father who he really was, and he was in danger of losing Ko-ko-mik-e-is if he did not.

"Why are you so sad?" Morning Star often asked his melancholy brother.

"Ah," sighed Anpao. "It is very difficult to explain it to you, Morning Star. I wish I could do so, but I cannot."

Morning Star became intrigued. "You promised to tell me everything," he exclaimed. "So don't hold anything back! Come, tell me, Scarface, why are you sad?"

"I cannot speak about it, Morning Star."

"If you will tell me," he whispered to Anpao, "if you tell me the story of your sadness, Scarface, I will tell you something very mysterious that I heard my father tell my mother."

"What is it?" Anpao asked, with renewed interest.

"Ah-ha! You must tell me and *then* I will tell you!" Morning Star said, laughing.

Anpao thought for a moment. He wanted to tell his brother the truth but he did not dare. "This much I will tell you: I am in love with a girl."

"Oh," Morning Star said in disappointment. "I thought it was going to be something exciting. Everybody is always in love with a girl! There is no adventure in that."

"But all the adventures of my life come from this one love for this beautiful girl. That is what is so mysterious about the story. Don't you understand?"

"I understand perfectly," Morning Star said, and laughed. "I have made love to the girls of your people too. They always cry and want you to stay with them forever. They are foolish and they are also faithless—though they seem to always talk about fidelity. And so are your men. They are always saying 'I love you' when they are with a girl, but as soon as they are away, they run after the next girl who comes along. Oh, I know all about this *love* of yours! It is foolishness, Anpao!" And Morning Star laughed.

"Yes, it might be foolish. I admit it. I do not really know Ko-ko-mik-e-is. I am not certain she even remembers me."

"Just as I told you, it is foolishness!"

"And she will never take me while I have this scar on my face," Anpao murmured sadly.

"Do you mean to say that this girl of yours loves you so little that she won't live with you because you have a scar on your face?" scoffed Morning Star.

"No, no, that is not the reason," Anpao answered, but then he stopped trying to clarify his predicament to Morning Star. What was the use? He could not admit his identity, and without that nothing made any sense.

"Now," Anpao said, hoping to change the subject, "I

have told you my secret. So it is your turn, Morning Star. What did you hear your father tell your mother that is so important?"

"Oh, that wasn't a real secret! I don't think it deserves something in exchange as mysterious as what I have to tell you."

"Come along, Morning Star, you gave me your word!"

"All right, then, I will tell you." He beckoned Anpao to come closer and then said in a cautious whisper, "I have heard marvelous things of a new people."

"What!"

"Shhhh!"

"All right, all right, but tell me, what new people?"

"If you will keep your voice down, Scarface, I will tell you!"

"All right," Anpao whispered in exasperation. "But don't be all day about it!"

"Shhh!"

"All right, all right."

Then Morning Star began again, "I have heard marvelous things about a new people who have come from far away. They are very strange. For one thing these people are as pale as my mother. Yes, that is true, for I heard my father speak of it. And they wear much hair about their mouths. It makes them look like one of our dogs running away with a black squirrel in his mouth!" Then they laughed. "Shhh!" Morning Star cautioned Anpao again. "My mother will be very angry if she knows that I have listened to their conversation."

"What else?" Anpao asked excitedly. "Who are these people with hair on their mouths?"

"I have heard that they are already despised by many of your people. But though these strangers are despised for some things, for others they are admired as being very powerful. I have learned that they have made a marvelous fireboat. That is how they came from out of the great water. It is this fireboat that carried them across the water. I do not understand it. How have they combined things which cannot exist together? Either the water would put out their fires, or else the fire would consume their boats. But their fireboats do not burn down and the water is so frightened that it does not put out their fires!"

"Is this the truth?" exclaimed Anpao.

"I swear to you, it is what my father told my mother when he had come home from a long journey to the East. He said that these Big Knives, as he calls them, have made a fireboat-walks-on-mountains. That is what the new people have made!"

"But what is this fireboat-walks-on-mountains?" urged Anpao.

"I will tell you," said Morning Star. "Those who have seen this monster say that it flies from mountain to mountain when it gets excited. They say that it carries the thunderbird, for it frequently makes the bird's great war whoop, and it puffs fire and smoke when it is excited! However, I understand that this fireboat-walks-on-mountains cannot move except on the trail made for it by the Big Knives."

"Ah! In that case it could not chase after us into rough country! So it is possible to escape from it!"

"That is right. It cannot chase you over rocks," Morning Star agreed, much to Anpao's relief.

"What are these strangers called? Do they have a name?"

"This I do not know. My father called them Big Knives, for they have come with something unlike the sharp rock-blades of our spears and axes. It is called 'iron' and is something my father has known and kept secret since the beginning of the world. These Big Knives somehow learned the secret and have made this precious iron into many marvelous things. They do many wonders with it. They also do other strange things. They divide the day into hours, like the moons of the year. In fact, they measure everything. Not one of them would let so much as a turnip go from his garden unless he counted it.

"All of this is true. They are very strange. They have many children for peculiar reasons that I cannot understand. My father said that he saw one of them with no less than nine children! And I understand that there are great men among them and these men give feasts and invite many people, but when the feast is over the guests are required to pay for what they have eaten before they are permitted to leave. They are both foolish and wise, and even my father does not know for certain whether they are monsters or men."

Anpao studied Morning Star's face for a long time as the two young men sat in astonished silence. "I cannot believe that you are telling me the truth," Anpao said.

"It is true, Scarface. It is just as I have told it."

"And these Big Knives—will they also come here?"

"My father," Morning Star whispered, "told my mother that since they had found the secret of iron they could go anywhere. They are like fishes and birds and buffaloes all in one. They spread like the clouds in a rainy sky, covering everything. And they have a terrible weapon that drives back everything that comes in front of it. It is a hollow rod that makes a terrifying noise and hurls a lump of iron so swiftly that the eye cannot follow its flight and with such force that it can kill any animal or man at a distance!"

"Ah," sighed Anpao, staring first at Morning Star and then into the distance. He was thinking of the village of Ko-ko-mik-e-is and fearing that perhaps these terrible Big Knives had already spread across the great prairie and trampled the village and all its people—killing them with the hollow-rods-with-fire.

"Your people are afraid of these strangers," Morning Star said softly. "They are full of fear because the Big Knives want everything they see. It is a disease they have, for like little ants they must pick up and carry off everything they see—even things much bigger than they are. They can leave nothing where they find it but must carry everything away."

"Ah," sighed Anpao. In the distance, for the first time, he could hear in the wind the sounds of weeping. He could hear from every direction the weeping that spread across the land. In the wind a voice was calling: "Oh, my children, we must go far away. Oh, my children, where can I take you?"

In the days when Anpao lived with the Sun, people had to walk wherever they went. Their dogs could carry light burdens, but people had to carry everything else. Now they were fleeing from the Big Knives, packing their possessions and walking vast distances to escape the white-skinned people who had come from the water.

"The people cannot escape the fireboat-walks-on-mountains. They must have help if they are to escape," Anpao murmured with great distress.

"If you promise me that you will not say a single word about it," Morning Star whispered to Anpao, "I will show you something miraculous."

"No miracle is great enough to help me now," Anpao groaned.

"But it is," Morning Star insisted. "This miracle is so powerful it could even stop the Big Knives!"

"Then tell me quickly what it is," Anpao begged.

"First swear to me that you won't tell my father or mother anything about it, because if they knew that I have found out their secret they would be very angry."

"All right! All right! I swear it! But what is it and where can I see it?"

"Shhh! That is what I am trying to tell you if you will only be silent for a moment so I can talk!"

"Yes, yes, tell me, but do it quickly because you always take too long with your stories and that makes me become impatient!"

"It is on the other side of the lake . . ."

"Where the terrible birds live?" Anpao interrupted.

"Yes, that is where it is."

"Then we must forget about it," Anpao said resolutely.

"It is forbidden for us to go near the big water where the birds are."

"It will be all right. Please, Scarface, trust me. It will be all right."

"No. It is forbidden," Anpao said again, "and I have given the Moon my word that I would not let you go near the birds."

"But don't you want to see what my father has brought back from the Big Knives?" Morning Star asked with a smirk on his face.

"Did your father bring back a fireboat?" Anpao exclaimed.

"It is something more wonderful," Morning Star said, and laughed. "But you can't see it unless we go to the big water, because that is where I saw my father put it just so it would be far out of sight. He has fooled us, I'm certain of it, for that is the only reason it is forbidden to go near the water."

"That is not true, Morning Star, and I know it. The Moon told me that the birds have killed all of your brothers and would also kill you and any other son of the Sun. So don't try to trick me into hunting those birds, because I can see through your guile and I refuse to do it!"

"Does that mean that you do not want to see the magic dogs?" Morning Star asked nonchalantly, as he got up and walked slowly in the direction of the water. Anpao hurried along behind him.

"Magic dogs? What magic dogs?"

"Well, it's no use discussing the matter, because you say

you refuse to go near the birds or the water, and that's exactly where my father put the magic dog he stole from the Big Knives," Morning Star said coyly.

"All right! All right! Perhaps I was too hasty about my decision, Morning Star. But you must first tell me what the magic dog is and then we can discuss whether it is safe to go by the water and take a look at it."

Morning Star smiled victoriously and sat down. After a very long silence, he told the story of the magic dog.

"My father was visiting one of the places where your people live. He saw a man come out of his tipi, who stretched and yawned as he did every morning. Then the man saw something that made him give a tremendous hoot. Well, all the people came running to see what he had seen. In the distance there was a herd of dogs coming toward the village, but they were dogs unlike any the people had ever seen before. First of all, they were too large to be dogs. Their legs were too long and their tails hung down lifelessly rather than standing up and wagging properly. When these magic dogs came very close, all the dogs of the village came running out of their tipis and barked and tried to chase these strange new animals away. But the magic dogs kicked with their back feet and rose up and tried to trample the dogs with their front feet. Well, the men were amazed and the women grabbed the children and ran back into their shelters. At first the men laughed at the foolish women for being afraid, but then even the men became frightened when these strange magic dogs began to split themselves in two! The top part got down off the bottom part and stood on the ground just like a man would. That was the magic! Because when the top got down, what was left was an animal with four long legs which looked just like a very big dog. They were magic dogs!

"Well," Morning Star continued, "the part that looked like a man opened its mouth and repeatedly pointed down its throat with its finger. The villagers waited to see what would come out but nothing did. So they shook their heads, because they couldn't understand what was happening. Then the part that looked like a man rubbed its stomach and opened and closed its mouth as if it was chewing. 'Aha,' the people said. 'Maybe it wants something to eat. What do you think it eats?' Well, nobody knew for certain what such a strange creature would want to eat. 'Maybe it eats meat and bones as dogs do,' someone suggested. So one of the women ran off to get some meat, when suddenly the lower part of the animal began to eat grass. 'Ah, he wants grass!' So the children ran off to get as much grass as they could gather. Well, the bottom part liked the grass, but the top part was still pointing down its throat with its finger. 'I think maybe we should try dog food again,' a woman insisted, and she presented the animal with a large bone. But nothing seemed to please the creature. Now it kept pointing at the fire. '*Nosotros somos Españoles*,' said the one that looked like a man. '*Carne cocida, por favor.*' It sounded like nothing anyone had ever heard before. Well, finally one of the creatures took the meat and held it over the fire. 'They want it cooked!' a woman shouted. And so they fed the bottom part grass, and the top part cooked meat."

Anpao gazed incredulously at Morning Star. "Do you mean to tell me that your father brought one of these magic dogs back here?" he exclaimed with excitement.

"Not the whole animal. That is the trouble," Morning Star apologized. "Because it seems that the top part is not as cooperative as the bottom. And so my father only managed to bring back the bottom half."

"And what does this magic dog look like?" Anpao asked.

"I will show it to you, if you will be reasonable about the birds that live near the water. We can easily kill the birds if we use the iron weapons which my father has hidden in our lodge. And then you can see the magic dogs for yourself!"

"All right," Anpao said reluctantly. "We will try, but, Morning Star, if anything happens to you, your father and mother will surely kill me and they will have good reason to do so!"

Morning Star was much pleased to have his way. Before Anpao could say anything more, he ran off to fetch the iron weapons from the lodge.

The Battle with the Birds

—————◆—————

The Sun was hidden behind the tiers of clouds that boiled slowly in the tumultuous sky. The land flattened itself against the horizon, leaving only the long lean valley of the forbidden lake where the birds made their curious wailing.

Despite Anpao's constant warnings, Morning Star hurried toward the shore. He knew nothing of the dangers of the world. "Be careful, Morning Star!" Anpao warned, as he tried to catch up with his impatient brother.

"There is nothing to fear," Morning Star said, and laughed foolishly.

But Anpao could feel the danger that surrounded the mysterious silver water where thin yellow whiffs of smoke rose and twisted into the vacant gray air.

"If these birds are so dangerous," said Morning Star, "why is it that we can't even see them?"

"Ah." Anpao shuddered as he peered closely into the dense haze that encircled them as they approached the luminous water. "That is the most dangerous sign of all."

Morning Star laughed. "Anpao, I think you're afraid of little birds!"

"I am afraid of birds I cannot see . . ."

This made Morning Star laugh even louder. But his laughter lasted only a moment, for the sky suddenly cried out and split open like a pomegranate. The clouds turned red and tumbled violently down upon the water, which began to boil. "Ah!" Morning Star trembled as he clutched Anpao. But before he could speak, the air was filled with horrendous screeching, and an entire mountain far above them splintered into thunderous boulders, which came crashing through the gash in the sky and plummeted into the fiery lake, throwing up torrents of burning mud and ash.

Then there was silence.

All that could be heard was the breathing of the two young men who stood in the dense fog which blotted out everything except the crimson glow that rose from the seething lake.

They could see nothing. They could hear nothing. The forest, the lodge of the Sun, the distant mountains and desert . . . everything had vanished except the endless veils of radiant mist that surrounded them.

Morning Star made a dreadful little sound. Anpao was afraid to look into his face for fear of what he might see there. Morning Star made the stifled sound again, and when Anpao fearfully glanced at him he saw that he was smiling.

"Why do you laugh at a time like this?"

But Morning Star did not answer. His laughter grew louder until he was half crazy with mirth. As he roared and sank to his knees, he waved his arms wildly in the air and seemed to be pointing at something above.

"What is it?" Anpao whispered urgently, not knowing

whether Morning Star was mad or playing a game. "Please, Morning Star, stop acting the fool and tell me what the matter is!"

Morning Star tried to respond, but he could not control his laughter. "See . . . look . . ." He laughed hysterically, as he pointed into the air.

"Ah!" Anpao exclaimed in terror, fearing that Morning Star had been attacked by the birds and was dying. But when he tried to lift his brother to his feet, he was helpless and could do nothing. All this while, Morning Star kept pointing with uncontrolled gestures into the empty sky.

Then Anpao saw them. There were two, three . . . perhaps six . . . very, very small, yellow birds. And that was all. They were flitting over the boys' heads and chirping so feebly that their sound was hardly audible.

"See, see . . . do you see, Anpao?" Morning Star asked. "Do you see the terrible, terrible birds we have to fight?" He roared with laughter as he imitated the tiny chirping birds and hopped about making tiny bird sounds. "Are these the monsters my mother says will kill me?"

Anpao was not as quick to be amused by the birds. "Yes, Morning Star," he said seriously. "I can see them. They are very little birds . . . and they are surely harmless. But, Morning Star, perhaps there are also things here which we cannot see," he whispered.

"Oh, Anpao, please! Don't be so gloomy all the time!" Morning Star scoffed as he brushed the dust from his leggings. "There is no danger from these tiny yellow birds, my dear friend. You can see that just by using your eyes. Come on now, let's go quickly and see the magic dog before my mother and father miss us!"

"Please, Morning Star, be careful. Sometimes our eyes are not enough." But Morning Star ignored the warning and hurried toward the edge of the water.

"There!" Morning Star called jubilantly. He pointed into the misty distance where Anpao could vaguely see the outline of an immense doglike creature grazing peacefully on the other side of the lake.

But at the same moment the air thundered again. "KAAAAH!" came a fantastic cry. And Anpao looked up just as one of the tiny yellow birds spread its enormous black wings and its eyes flashed red.

From all around the boys there was a rush of wings and a fierce outcry. They fell to the ground and—*chop!*—something absolutely enormous swooped down and tore a great gash in the earth just next to where Morning Star was cowering. Anpao rushed toward his brother, waving his ax in the air, though he could not see what it was that had attacked them.

Chop!

Again there was a terrific rush of huge wings and a terrifying snarl as something swooped down and tore an entire tree from the swampy ground, carrying it up into the air before letting it come crashing back down.

Anpao grabbed Morning Star and dragged the paralyzed boy along as fast as he could. The roar in the air was like a hundred hurricanes and Anpao could barely stagger forward. The great gusts of wind swirled about them as huge wings struck Anpao in the head and repeatedly knocked him down. He could feel an immense beak slash past his body like a fiercely sharp ax. Then another rush of wings swept him to the ground, missing the boys' bodies by the slightest distance and ripping a tree in two.

"Run! Morning Star, run!" Anpao shouted desperately, as he slashed the air with his weapons and tried to work his way under the protective ledge of a great boulder. "Run, run, Morning Star, run quickly! Don't wait for me—run!"

In a daze Morning Star scrambled to his feet with a look of utter dread and began to run without knowing where to run or what was chasing him. Anpao crouched under the rock and prayed to all the powerful spirits of the world and of the sky. When he opened his eyes he could not see the attacking monsters, but at least Morning Star was still alive and running in frenzied circles. He prayed again, harder than he had ever prayed. Then he jumped to his feet and, taking a deep breath, he opened his eyes.

The mist was gone! Looking into the bright sky above poor Morning Star, Anpao could see the astonishing creatures that were swooping down upon his brother. At last he could see them!

He drew his weapons and raced toward his brother with the loudest war cry anyone had ever uttered. "WHOOOP!" he shouted, making a thunder almost as great as that of the terrible birds.

The tiny yellow birds were in the air—but they were only decoys riding on the beaks of gigantic beings with the barbed wings of bats. The great heads of these creatures were long and pointed and their immense mouths were lined with row upon row of glistening little teeth. As the monsters plummeted again and again toward the terrified Morning Star, who could not see them, their wings beat furiously and their vicious mouths tore huge wounds into the earth around the frightened boy.

Anpao pushed Morning Star to the ground and stood over him, slicing the air with his iron weapons. Morning Star still could not see the attackers, but Anpao could see them perfectly. His weapons ruptured their enormous wings and knocked countless teeth from their gaping mouths. Again and again they swept past the young man and then withdrew in wide circles in the sky.

One by one Anpao wounded the great birds, but they did not bleed as other animals bleed. Instead their wounds pulsated with sparks and burning coals. The wounded monsters whirled into the sky in dizzy loops and then they burst into flames and, with pathetic cries, they streaked upward and farther upward into the sky.

As the monsters ascended, the world began to darken. The sky turned black and utterly silent as their screams faded into the heights. "Ah," cried Morning Star. "The Sun is dying! A snake has come up from under the world and is swallowing my father! Anpao, what have I done to my great father?"

Then suddenly the stars began to fall. All the lights in the sky spun and sputtered. They streaked in every direction in the great blackness of the sky. "The stars are falling!" Morning Star shouted in delirium. "The sky is falling!"

But it was not the sky . . . it was the entire race of monster birds dying and falling like meteors from the sky. One after another they burst into a shower of sparks and plummeted to the ground. It didn't seem as if there would be any stars left in the sky. But then at last the shower stopped.

It was darker than any night of the world. But it was not night. There was no Sun or Moon and there were no stars.

While Morning Star crouched in the terrible darkness, Anpao slowly rose and began to make music by striking his iron weapons against each other. And he began to dance and to sing, throwing back his head and chanting with great passion in his voice. He danced and he danced. He sang and he sang. Soon a tiny rim of light began to appear in the sky —no bigger than the edge of a fingernail. Anpao danced harder and sang louder and louder. The light in the sky grew larger and larger, until the whole blazing Sun slowly came back into the sky and the world was alive again. It was the year when for the first time the Sun and the Moon appeared together in the sky.

The Moon was waiting when Morning Star and Anpao staggered home exhaustedly. "The birds!" she groaned, as she hurried to Morning Star to make certain that he was not wounded. "You have been attacked by the birds despite all my warnings!"

She rushed into the lodge, pulling the dazed Morning Star after her, and she bathed his wounds and put him to bed. And when Morning Star confessed what they had done and told her how Anpao had saved his life, she was very happy. She cried and embraced the astonished Anpao and called him "my son."

That night when the Sun came home, the Moon told him what had happened, and he too was very grateful. "Scarface, you may be only a person, but you are as wise and powerful as those of us who live in the sky. Henceforth I will call you *son!*"

When the Sun said this Anpao wept.

"So tell me, my son, what can I do to repay your great bravery?"

"*Hai-yu!*" exclaimed the happy Anpao. "Pity me, Father. I ask you only one thing."

"What is it?"

"It is this scar—I would like you to remove it from my face."

"It is difficult, what you ask of me. But you are good and I have promised to give you what you want." And so, with a motion of his golden fingers, the Sun took the scar from Anpao's face. He was transformed at once. The Sun, the Moon, and Morning Star stared at him in amazement, for he looked exactly like his celestial brother and his great father. He was very handsome and tall and his body was perfectly formed and heavily muscled.

"Ah," murmured the Sun, as he looked closely into Anpao's beautiful face. "Your face is very familiar now that your scar is gone . . ."

Anpao smiled at his father. At once the Sun understood everything and happily embraced his lost son. The Moon, however, did not guess Anpao's identity. But she grew to love him and always thought of him as her earth-person-son, Scarface. So Anpao became the first person in whom the power of the Sun, the Moon, and the Earth of his mother were united.

"Scarface is wise and good and he is also brave," the Moon told her family. "From today he will be my son and the brother of Morning Star!"

The Sun winked at Anpao and said, "That is just as it should be."

Anpao was now ready for his long journey home to Ko-ko-mik-e-is. Morning Star and the Sun had given him many beautiful presents—the handsomest weapons any human person had ever owned; the magic dog, which Anpao named Horse; the precious emblems of the Sun and the Moon, to show that Anpao and his people were at peace with them forever; and elegant clothes like none anyone on earth had ever beheld.

The Sun and Morning Star were sad to say good-by to Anpao. But it was the Moon, once his terrible enemy, who cried the hardest and kissed him many times and called him "my son" when he prepared to leave the lodge of the Sun.

The Moon stood by the doorway of the lodge and took from her hair two feathers of the Raven. "Keep these feathers as a sign for a beautiful girl in your world. They must always be worn by the husband of the woman who builds a medicine lodge, which you will teach your people to build so that it resembles the lodge of the Sun."

Then the Sun showed Anpao a shortcut which would help him find his way home quickly. It was called the Wolf Road, or the Milky Way. After embracing the Moon and his brother Morning Star and his father the Sun, Anpao looked sadly at his family for the last time and turned toward the long trail that twisted earthward among the vast glittering beadwork of the stars.

He Comes from the East

———◆———

It was a hot day. Anpao had ridden his marvelous Horse very far, hoping he might find a friendly village where he could make camp and get something to eat. He traveled on and on but he saw no sign of his people. Finally at midday he came upon a cluster of lodges. The people sat listlessly in the shade sleeping. All the lodge skins were raised to let the air in, and all the cooking fires had gone out. No one heard Anpao ride into camp until a chief suddenly awakened and shouted in surprise to see such an elegant warrior astride a magic animal.

Anpao greeted the people warmly, but they were selfish and unfriendly. They stared enviously at Anpao's possessions, and they peered at his horse. When he asked if they would share their food with him and give him shelter for the night, they only giggled and looked from one to another, each expecting someone else to be hospitable. But no one spoke up. All they could think about were devious ways of getting his belongings and his magic animal.

"If you will not share your food and fire with me, I will ride on until I find people who are kind to strangers," Anpao told them.

"Oh, no," the musty old chief said with a false smile, as he rubbed his chin and gazed at Anpao's weapons and clothes. "You are welcome to share our fire, but we cannot give you any food unless you give us something in return." Then the chief bowed awkwardly and smiled his toothless smile. He insisted that Anpao stay in the village and he offered him a bone which none of the dogs of the camp would have eaten. Anpao frowned at the repulsive chief, whose face was full of ignorance and whose body was deformed from eating garbage and from sloth and idleness. He pushed away the hand which extended the rancid bone to him. Anpao could see the selfish hearts of these people and he knew that their falseness was a new disease, which had taken hold of the lowest of the human creatures who lived at the rim of the world where the Milky Way ascended to his father's home. In their disfigured faces he could see their avarice, and he knew that they wanted to detain him only so they might overpower him at night and steal his possessions. But he did not fear them, for he pitied their ignorance and he knew that the Sun, the Moon, and Morning Star would protect him against such monsters. So he accepted their fire and nothing more.

After the people of the barbarous village had gobbled their food sullenly in the secrecy of dark corners of their lodges, they came out into the night where Anpao was sitting with dignity near the fire. They gazed at his beautiful possessions and cautiously approached the great animal.

"What do you call your monster?" the chief asked in a whining voice.

"He is a friend, not a monster. His name is Horse."

"Ahuh, so it is. So it is." The old chief nodded, rubbing his gray face with his nubby hands and making no effort to disguise the greed in his little eyes, except for the dreadful oily smile he occasionally flashed at Anpao.

"Horse, you say. Ahuh. Well, it is a very powerful person, this Horse. And valuable. If we had such a Horse we could make all our enemies run for their lives and never come back again!"

And the old chief cackled. Then he drew close to Anpao and grinned into his face, whispering, "I will tell you a secret, young fellow. Tomorrow morning we intend to attack our enemies who live in a village not far from here. We intend to kill them." And he cackled again. "We intend to carry away their possessions and their women. And their children will work for us and we will eat all their dogs!" The old chief shook with wheezing while he panted his terrible breath into Anpao's face.

"Now," the chief whined, tilting his misshapen head to the side so his motley hair fell across his face, "if you were to come with us—on your monster...ah, that would make our victory certain! And," he wheezed, "I would give you a whole dog to yourself for doing it!"

Anpao looked away. "No," he said calmly. "I have no enemies here and I will not help you fight people I do not even know. Besides, I am very tired and I want to sleep now. In the morning I will leave your camp before you and your war party return."

Then Anpao left the man as quickly as he could. He

had been away from his people for so long that he had forgotten they could be so lowly.

He searched for the most secluded place near the fire. The people mumbled unintelligibly and cleared a path for him, peering at him all the while. Then, as he tried to fall asleep, he could hear the people whispering. But he was not afraid. He knew that they were cowards and were too much afraid of his friend Horse and of his powerful weapons to approach his bed while he slept. So he closed his eyes and dreamed of Ko-ko-mik-e-is.

In the morning Anpao awakened to find the camp deserted, for the people had gone off to attack their enemies. He packed his possessions quickly and gave Horse grass and water and was about to leave the village when he heard the sounds of war whoops. He was surprised that the people were returning so soon, for surely their enemies could not have been destroyed so easily.

The excited people ran into the camp. All of them were talking at the same time. Apparently the village scouts had watched the enemy camp from a knoll all through the night, but they had seen absolutely no activity. They feared their wily enemies and suspected they might be luring them into a clever trap. The villagers told the scouts to go down into the valley and try to see what the enemies were doing. At dawn the scouts did as they were told, and when they returned they said that they still could see no one in the camp, though they had approached very near. So, while Anpao had slept, the villagers attacked the silent enemy encampment, ripping open the lodge covers with their stone axes and spears and preparing to pounce upon their enemies and destroy them all.

But there was no one to fight. The people in the lodges were dead or dying. There was no one able to fight, for every man, woman, and child in the camp was covered with something fearsome that no one had ever seen on a person's body before.

The village people believed that an evil power had destroyed their enemies for them. Joyfully, they collected everything in sight—the best lodges, the camp equipment—and they burned everything that remained. Then they hurried back to their own village to celebrate their victory and the scalps they had taken.

"We did not have to fight a single man. The spirits did it for us!" the old chief cackled as he pulled around his deformed body a fur that he had stolen.

Anpao wanted nothing more to do with these people. Even Horse began to whinny nervously as he backed away from the stench of the possessions taken from the enemies, stomping his feet violently and shaking his elegant head. Anpao sensed the danger too, and, without saying anything more, he quickly mounted and hurried away.

The Horse and Anpao raced through the lowlands as fast as Horse could run, for there were bad signs everywhere. In the night the Moon did not come into the sky, and when Anpao made camp his humble fire did not want to burn, but sent long, mournful trails of smoke into the silent darkness above.

All during the night the great Horse-friend whinnied

and stamped his feet nervously as if something evil were coming. And in the morning Anpao hurried to be on his way, more anxious than ever to reach the village of Ko-ko-mik-e-is, for he feared that something terrible was coming upon the whole world.

At midday he saw a tiny village in the distance, far across the desolate flatland which was the last, vast barrier between him and the mountain where Ko-ko-mik-e-is lived with her people. Hoping that perhaps the village would be occupied by generous people who would give him food and water, Anpao gently coaxed Horse forward. But as they neared the village, there was a silence as terrible and deep as the one the chief had described in the camp of his enemies. The Sun burned down on the lodges whose linings flapped vacantly in the aimlessness of the wind. A cloud of dust hung over the camp and there was no sound except the occasional growling of dogs from somewhere behind the lodges. When Anpao reached the center of the village he was horrified by what he found. Great was the stench of the dead. The fathers and the grandfathers had succumbed where they lay, and the rest of the people had fled into the endless desert. Only the starving dogs remained, and they fought with the vultures for the dead bodies, which they dragged into the shadows where they devoured them.

Horse suddenly reared up, shook his head violently, and dashed quickly away, while Anpao clung to his wild mane and stared back in disbelief at the horrid scene. There could be no more lucky days now. The people were dying. Something terrible had come upon the world, and no one was safe. Not the people of the land, not Anpao, not even Ko-ko-mik-e-is.

With that thought Anpao shouted into the sky with desperation and fled with his Horse-friend toward the village of his beloved.

Horse was very tired now and walked painfully and slowly over the dusty flatland. There was no water anywhere and still the lifeless land stretched ceaselessly before them. Though Anpao had come this way when he had left the home of Ko-ko-mik-e-is to seek the Sun, he recognized nothing from those days of his youth.

The world was changed. Where the deer had leaped across the grass, there was now a gray land with scattered herds of strange animals with white faces. The great river which once ran abundantly with clear water was soggy with sludge and rust. The air was filled with ash, and the spirits of the trees had abandoned their homes and left only the gnarled husks of leafless trunks. The antelope had vanished, and so too had the birds of the sky. No glistening white tipis rose against the vast blue sky; the sky was gray and the tipis were gone. There were no people, and all the fires had gone out.

"The end of the world has come," Anpao murmured. "The world in which I live is dying and soon my people will also be gone. I must hurry and find Ko-ko-mik-e-is before it is too late!"

As Anpao turned toward the distant mountain home of Ko-ko-mik-e-is, he saw something very far off. It was only a dark spot moving slowly toward him from the East—far across the vast void of the lowland.

"I do not understand," Anpao whispered. "It is from the East that new life comes. What comes from the East always dances with joy. It does not come slowly in a cloud of dust. I do not understand this thing which comes as slowly as death comes to an old man."

Anpao continued in the direction of the village of Ko-ko-mik-e-is, but as he went along he noticed that the thing way out there, whatever it might be, was going in the same direction. It frightened him and he urged Horse to walk a bit faster despite his fatigue.

As they went along, the thing grew larger and larger, and after a long while Anpao could see that it seemed to be a man on another magic dog. But this horse was a dismal creature. The red dust of the lowland covered it and it was very skinny and its head hung low. Red dust also clung to the man's clothes, a peculiar costume of black that covered his entire body like a sack, with black leggings reaching to his hips and a black sack about his chest and back and arms. The man was black everywhere except for a little white collar which made a perfect ring about his neck. The stranger's face was entirely covered by the red dust, except where motley hairs hung from the mouth and chin in a most peculiar manner.

As the man drew closer, Anpao could see that behind the dust on his face were countless sores and carbuncles, which ran with pus. Hundreds of tiny white worms rustled noisily around the man's throat and scrambled out of the light, slipping under his collar and disappearing as Anpao approached.

This terrible stranger drew rein and sat on his emaciated black roan horse. The animal's bones protruded from his sides and his head hung very low. His hoofs were festering with sores, and patches of fur were missing from his flaky hide. Now and again he made a sound that resembled the rattle in the throat of the dying.

"What is your name?" the stranger asked, as he sat placidly in his putrefaction, gazing at Anpao through watery eyes.

"My name is Anpao. I am to be the husband of Ko-ko-mik-e-is."

"I have never heard of you," the stranger muttered, "and I have never heard of Ko-ko-mik-e-is."

"I am the son of the Sun," Anpao said.

"Such stories do not interest me. I have never heard of you or Ko-ko-mik-e-is. Who is she?"

"She is the woman I will marry," Anpao said. "Now tell me, who are you, stranger?"

"I am Smallpox," the man said.

"Well, I have never heard of you either. Where do you come from and what do you do?"

"I come from very far away . . . from there—" and he pointed with a gray hand toward the East—"where the great water is and then far beyond it. I am a friend of the Big Knives who have brought me; they are my people."

"Ah," Anpao said. "But what is it you do for these Big Knives?"

"I bring death," Smallpox said, raising his hand and wiping the dust from his face so Anpao could see the sores that covered it. For a moment Anpao could not look at the man. Then he asked, "Do all the people you visit die?"

"Yes, all," said Smallpox.

"I think I have seen some of your work," Anpao whispered.

"Yes, all die . . . even your people, and your Ko-ko-mik-e-is too. Where do your people live? Why don't you invite me to come home with you? Sooner or later everyone will come to know me. If you will take me to your village I will spare your life, even though you have seen my face. But if you do not lead me to your village, then I will breathe on you and that will be the end."

Anpao could not bear the reek of death that surrounded the man. But he smiled and tried desperately to make an appearance of friendship so he could gain time and escape. Now he understood all that he had seen in the villages of the dead and dying where Old Man Smallpox had already visited.

"Well, I will tell you this," Anpao said, as nonchalantly as possible. "My people are rather ugly and they are hardly worth your effort. You are obviously a very great power and you surely want to visit only the most important villages where the people have much to live for. You don't have time to bother with people like my poor people."

"I always have time. No village is too much trouble for me," Smallpox said softly. "I will go with you and I will visit your village."

"Oh," Anpao said quickly, "but I am not going to my village. You see, I am on my way to hunt."

Smallpox gazed at Anpao dubiously, and then nodded his dreadful head. "If that is the case, then tell me, what is the way to your village? Tell me and I will let you go on your way."

"I will gladly tell you that. It is there—just where you see the trail I have left over the flatland. Just follow my trail and at the edge of this plain you will find my village."

"Good." Smallpox smiled as he picked up his reins. "Now hurry along and don't look back or I will forget my promise and breathe on you! However, my friend, don't be too happy. One day I will catch you too." Then Smallpox started along his way.

Anpao watched as the death-horse limped across the dusty lowland, along the trail Anpao had left. Once Smallpox had disappeared into the dust of the distance, Anpao trembled with relief and took a deep breath. The smell of death was gone, but the shadow of the horse and the man, which had been cast upon the ground in front of Anpao, remained like a deadly blemish on the earth.

Then quickly Anpao turned away from Smallpox and toward the village of Ko-ko-mik-e-is. He urged his Horse-friend to run as fast as he could, for Smallpox would soon discover the trick and there was no time to lose.

The Village Beneath the Water

In the village of Ko-ko-mik-e-is the trees that had been saplings when Anpao left in search of the Sun had grown tall. Many people had grown old and many new people had been born. Everything was changing, but Ko-ko-mik-e-is was the same. All of her friends had forgotten about Anpao and his promise to return. All the young men were now men, and they had stopped chasing Ko-ko-mik-e-is and married other girls. The boys who had grown to be young men ignored Ko-ko-mik-e-is. They called her "Old Girl," because of all the village women she alone was unmarried. They were sure that Anpao would never come back and that Ko-ko-mik-e-is was a fool.

Though she did not admit her sorrow, not even to her old father who was now chief of his people, Ko-ko-mik-e-is also feared that Anpao had forgotten her. She stayed inside her lodge day and night, venturing out only when her father asked her to bring water or wood. She did not dance with the young people and she did not sit with the girls and talk about marriage and children.

Her father, the chief, was a generous and gentle man, and he understood the sorrow that was concealed in Ko-ko-

mik-e-is's heart. So he was kind to her and never mentioned
that she was beyond the age when girls marry and that her
chances of having a husband were not what they had once
been when every young man wanted to marry her. The chief
hushed the women when they whispered about Old Girl
and he scolded the girls who giggled when they told stories
about the boy with the scar, Anpao, and how he had abandoned Ko-ko-mik-e-is and run off to marry a beautiful girl
from a distant tribe.

"Pay no attention, my daughter," the chief would
murmur sweetly to his sad child. "There are ways in your
heart that these foolish people do not understand. You must
follow your ways, no matter how difficult, and you must make
loneliness a willing companion. Pay no attention to them,
for they have no ways of their own but follow like children
after others."

Ko-ko-mik-e-is embraced her old father, and then she
hurried to the river and there, within the luminous green
tent of willows, she wept.

Early one morning, the chief, who was too old to sleep
like other people, arose from his bed and came out into the
dewy mist that hung over the world. The frail first light of
the Sun fell in successive rainbows through the air, making
halos around the treetops and shimmering among the beads
of dew that clung to the tall grass. Here in the high hills
of the village of Ko-ko-mik-e-is the earth was still new and
the animals strolled between the russet trunks of the tall
pines and there was everywhere the rustle and the fragrance
of pine needles and cedar bark. Birds made their elaborate

embroideries in the sky and filled the new day with songs. Sweet water dropped abundantly from rocks and ledges, trickling down the great slopes until the streams came together and tumbled over precipices and burst into white spray filled with rainbows and sunlight.

The old chief saw all this as he gazed contentedly into the new day. Then he noticed a person sitting way out on a butte at some distance from the village. This stranger sat silently, wrapped completely in his robe. All day he sat without moving. The girls came and went and the friends of the chief visited and feasted and smoked with him, but still the stranger sat silently on the butte. The Sun reached the middle of the sky and put on his golden headdress to dazzle the world, but still the stranger sat motionless in the heat, his robe wrapped around him. Then the Sun passed down toward the mountains, where he liked to linger at the end of the day, but still the stranger did not move.

When it was almost night, the chief said, "Why does that person sit there so long? Is he fasting and meditating or is he perhaps sick? The heat today has been very great, but this stranger has not eaten or taken any water. The heat was strong but the stranger sat wrapped in his winter robe. Perhaps he needs our help. Go and ask him to visit us and to share our food and our fire."

So two young men went to the stranger and said, "Why do you sit here in the great heat of day? Why do you sit here when it is night? Come to the lodge of our chief, who asks you to feast and to smoke with him."

Then the stranger arose and threw off his robe. The

young men were astonished. He wore the most beautiful clothes they had ever seen. His bow and shield were unlike any known to men. While one of the men was admiring these beautiful possessions, the other stared intently into the stranger's face, for he was certain he recognized the man.

"Ha!" he shouted with excitement. "Now I know who you are! It is the poor young man called Anpao! Look, he is poor no longer! And the scar has vanished from his face!"

All the people of the village came running to see if what they heard could be true. "Yes!" cried a very old woman. "I remember him well, for I made moccasins for him and his brother when they went in search of the Sun!"

"Tell us, Anpao, where have you been and what have you seen?" the young men begged him eagerly, as they admired his handsome stature and beautiful clothes. "Tell us, where did you get all of these beautiful things? Where have you been this long while and what have you seen on your journey?"

But Anpao did not answer. There in the crowd stood Ko-ko-mik-e-is. Anpao smiled at her and walked toward her, taking the two raven feathers from his head.

He gave them to her and then he said, "The trail was very long, and I nearly died. But with great Helpers and Powers I found the lodge of the Sun. He calls me son and he is glad. His wife, the Moon, also loves me and she sends these feathers to you. My brother, Morning Star, also sends his good wishes to you, for he has learned to be humble and he now loves the people of the world."

Ko-ko-mik-e-is wept with joy and all the people shouted and began to sing and to dance as the couple embraced and came down into the village where the old chief stood in front of his lodge with tears in his weary eyes. He was happier than anyone, for he had known all along that those who follow their own ways, even in the face of the bitterness of fools, are those in whom the Sun shines and to whom the mysteries of the Moon are known and the newness of the Morning Star radiates forever. He lifted his wand and stood taller than he had stood in many years, and he told his joyous people that he would give a wonderful feast for everyone.

"I am sorry, my good friend," Anpao told the chief sadly, "but we cannot sing and dance now. Something is coming . . . something terrible is coming to us. There is no time to celebrate now. Sickness and death and greed are coming down upon us. There is no time to delay. I have meditated long and asked my Power what we should do. Now I know how we can be saved, but there is little time. We must collect all that is ours and we must hurry away."

For a little while the people listened in fear, but then they quickly forgot their admiration for Anpao and treated him disrespectfully, as they had done when he had been a poor boy.

"Oh, there is no danger!" they assured him. "Nothing is going to happen to us. You have been sitting in the heat of the day too long," they said, and laughed. "Our holy people know everything there is to know and they tell us nothing of danger."

"There is no time," Anpao insisted. "If you do not trust me now, what good is all that I have done in order to make you believe in me?"

"Oh—" the people laughed again—"you are as crazy

as you were when you were poor and had a scar on your face!"

Anpao could not convince the people, no matter what he said to them. They looked around their beautiful village and the glorious forest and mountains filled with life and happiness and laughed at the notion that famine and death could come to such a perfect world.

"Stay here if you insist," Anpao told them. "But I cannot stay. I have seen what becomes of perfect worlds and I cannot be fooled by what I see, for I have learned to see more than what is before me." Then he turned to Ko-ko-mik-e-is and asked her gently, "Will you come with me?"

She smiled and did not have to answer.

That night the village slept without fear. They had feasted well and smoked to celebrate the marriage of Ko-ko-mik-e-is and Anpao and, having made many jokes about Anpao, they went off to their lodges.

But Ko-ko-mik-e-is and Anpao did not sleep. They gathered their belongings. Then Ko-ko-mik-e-is gently awakened her old father and begged him to come away with them.

The old man's eyes filled with sorrow as he looked at the two young people. "I would gladly go, yes, for I do believe in Anpao and, though I do not understand what he says, I trust his power. I always believed in him and knew he would return. And now I also believe that he knows what is good and wise for us. But, my children, I am old, and I am the chief of all these foolish people who only know laughter and wonderment. If I were to leave my people alone to face whatever is coming to us, it would be very wrong. They are like beautiful butterflies—how will they live if what you say is coming descends upon them? How can they bear the ugliness and the greed, they who are children of this fertile Earth and own nothing and give everything away as children do? No, my daughter and my new son, I cannot leave them.

"Besides, look at me. I am such a very old person now. If I were to go with you, I would walk too slowly and I would hold back your young legs which can spring to safety. No, my children, I cannot go. You are strong and young... go where you must go and go with my prayers. But I must remain here with all my other children."

The old chief embraced Ko-ko-mik-e-is. Then he pressed her from him sadly and gazed into the eyes of her new husband. "This is my only born child. I entrust her to you and I know it is with a man of power and vision that she walks now." Then he turned away so he would not see his daughter leave him.

Ko-ko-mik-e-is sobbed and ran with Anpao from the lodge. It was a dark and windy night as they traveled westward across the short grass of the little valley. On and on they journeyed until finally they came to a great water, larger, deeper, and clearer than any they had seen.

The spirits of the Raven and the Sun took Anpao's hand. The spirits of the Moon and those of Morning Star and the Kit-Fox took the hand of Ko-ko-mik-e-is. Together they chanted by the water and together they sang: "Come with us to safety in the village below."

"Ah," sighed Ko-ko-mik-e-is. "But if we follow you

we will surely die. Will this be the end of us and of all our people in this glorious world?"

"There is no end of us," Anpao whispered. "Do not be afraid. Our lives are like the rings of an ancient tree. We are the rivers and we are this land. We are the ancient ways of our fathers and of our fathers' fathers, from the days when the rivers were clear and the prairie was covered with buffaloes, when the giant redwoods were saplings in the first frail dawns of this vast land. Do not be afraid. We cannot die while these great things live within us. Under every rock of this land there is a trace of us. Do not be afraid. The buffaloes and all the dead will return. They will come with a great explosion and in a cloud of smoke. The fireboat-walks-on-mountains will bring the people back again, whooping joyously as they come to us, waving their arms and shouting victoriously. Do not be afraid, for the fireboat-walks-on-mountains will bring them back again. I know, for I have seen it!"

Then the song was over and in the silence of the night the spirits led Anpao and Ko-ko-mik-e-is slowly down into the beautiful water. For a moment Ko-ko-mik-e-is gasped with fear as the water touched her face, but she smiled and gazed at Anpao as they descended. Then they were gone.

"Ah, do you hear the voices? Do you hear the women laughing? Do you hear?"

The holy man Wasicong sat by the lake in the night, luminous in the light that rose from the blue water as he listened to the distant drums and to the singing of the drowned village.

"It is Ko-ko-mik-e-is and Anpao and all their children!" he whispered.

Then he pointed down into the Moon-filled water where shimmering images of liquid-people danced and leaped and rose like smoke on a clear night. "They possessed great power to go under the water. Without such power, we cannot join them. Without power, all of us must drown."

And then old Wasicong looked up into the perfect Moon and he smiled slowly as he rustled his cloak of ravens' feathers.

"Ah," he said. "That is the story of how the world began and how the boy Anpao was born and of his adventures among the people and among the spirits." And he winked his large yellow eyes and nodded.

"Ah . . ." Wasicong whispered, as he leaped into the air effortlessly and flew to the top of a pine tree that overlooked the water where the drowned village shimmered in the blue depths.

"Do you hear . . . do you hear their singing?"

> The Sun's beams are running out.
> The Sun's beams are running out.
> The Sun's golden rays are running out.
> We shall live again.
> We shall live again.

The Storyteller's Farewell

———◆———

Notes on Sources

———◆———

Bibliography

The Storyteller's Farewell

———————◆———————

Among American Indians the teller of stories is a weaver. His designs are the threads of his personal saga as well as the history of his people. Though the designs are always traditional, the hands that weave them are always new. These stories, like ancient Indian designs, have been passed from one generation to the next and sometimes have been borrowed by one tribe from another. None of the tales is my own invention; they were all born long before I came into the world. The words, like the threads of a weaving, are new, and these are mine, but the stories belong to everyone.

Some of these tales are very old, so old that no one knows quite when they originated. Others are quite recent, coming out of the experience of Indians since the white man invaded their country, bringing his industries, horses, firearms, and, sadly, diseases that were unknown in America before 1492. But old or new, the stories have no known authors. They exist as the river of memory of a people, surging with their images and their rich meanings from one place to another, from one generation to the next—the tellers and the told so intermingled in time and space that no one can separate them.

ANPAO

This book represents no single tribe, though many of the stories I have drawn upon come from the Northern Plains because that is the region of my own upbringing. Yet every narration in *Anpao* comes directly from the Native American heritage and very little has been invented in the sense that fiction is invented by a writer.

The character called Anpao is a fabrication. There is no such central Indian hero. In fact there is no pan-Indian history, for Indian cultures are far too diversified to accommodate a uniform view of history or to embrace a single cultural hero. I created Anpao out of many stories of the boyhood of early Indians, and from my own experience as well, in order to make an Indian "Ulysses" who could become the central dramatic character in the saga of Indian life in North America.

Anpao ventures through his own boyhood (a boyhood which comes essentially from Plains tradition, but also includes elements of Southwest customs). At the same time he also journeys through history, for *Anpao* is itself a kind of chronicle of the Indians of America, though it is folk history rather than the presumably objective history of white men. At the same time that Anpao journeys through Indian history he also travels across much of the face of his ancient world, encountering the deserts, mountains, and prairies of America and meeting many different tribes with diversified cultures and customs. In this way *Anpao* is able to encompass a good deal of the variety of tribal life in North America—the lands, the life-styles, the folk history. But the diversity of Indians is great. Indian versions of Genesis alone are so numerous that no one story can take all of the variations into account. Therefore the tales of *Anpao* are selected from a very large body of oral history, in much the way that Homer's tales in the *Odyssey* represent only a fragment of the tales of all the tribes of the Aegean.

North American Indians did not evolve a written language, at least not the kind of language familiar to the peoples of Europe. This book is my personal effort to use the vast facilities of the tradition of written literature to convey the energy, uniqueness, and imagery of Indian oral tradition. I have approached it, however, not as a stenographer or as an ethnologist, who would tend to value verbatim transcriptions. I have written these stories as a writer. But I have been careful to preserve the qualities unique to non-written folk history.

It is possible that readers will wonder what I have contributed to the stories of *Anpao* other than collecting them from countless tellers. I suspect I have done the same thing that many prior generations of tellers of history have done, only the creative process in my effort is much more like the methods used by contemporary Indian painters than the techniques of ancient storytellers. Like modern Indian painters I have made use of new potentials of technique and imagination which I have learned through the education available in the twentieth century. I believe, as do contemporary Indian painters, in the existence of some sort of transcendent Indian sensibility, and I believe that its power and its truth can be expressed in modes typical of our day as well as in the venerated, old style of the traditionalists.

Just as young Indian painters with a command of modern methods have reinterpreted Indian iconography and history in a new style, so I have recounted the stories I have heard all my life in a prose which tries to merge the old and the new.

I believe that there are images and ideas which are uniquely Indian and remain uniquely Indian no matter what mannerisms are employed to present them. These Indian ideas are central to the stories in *Anpao*. My aim has been to illuminate them as self-contained realities, without drawing parallels to non-Indian rationale or attempting to "apologize" for them or to "explain" them. I have presented these old tales neither as curiosities nor as naive fiction, but as an alternative vision of the world and as an alternative process of history.

You may have noticed that I am disinclined to refer to "myths" and "legends" when I talk about *Anpao*. This is because these words express the dominant society's disregard for the beliefs of other peoples, just as I would be expressing a nonchalant superiority were I to speak to Christians of their "Jesus myths." *Anpao* is not concerned with myth but with a reality which seems to have escaped the experience of non-Indians.

Since completing this book I have become aware of a literary movement among Indians of Latin America which is intent upon very much the same purposes as my efforts in *Anpao*. This South American literature is sometimes called Magic Realism, as opposed to Surrealism (with its self-conscious dream world) and to Naive Realism (with its pretentions to irrevocable factuality). Magic Realism is the outcome of the writing of Indians who are fully trained in both the language of the dominant civilization and the "otherness" of Indian culture. Thus the magic dogs which appear in a sequence of *Anpao* are neither "real" horses nor horses "distorted" by surrealistic mannerisms. The magic dogs are facts from another scheme of reality. They are not products of a lavish imagination but products of the vision of a people whose experience is fundamentally different from that of white civilization.

Most of the stories in *Anpao* exist in many versions. Since the turn of the century ethnologists have been very active in transcribing the stories, and they have sought the cooperation of various Indians (informants, as they call them) who allow their narratives to be transcribed or, more recently, to be reproduced on records or tape. I think it might be interesting to trace various versions of the stories I have recounted in *Anpao* and to discover the tribes in which the tales originated. Therefore I have assembled a list that identifies most of the tales, poems, songs, and events which occur in *Anpao*. I have also tried to indicate at least one book in which each tale can be read in its traditional, transcribed form.

There is not one of the stories which has not been told to me countless times since I was a boy—at powwows, among friends and family, and while traveling across America to do research for my books. But most of these stories have also been collected by ethnologists. There are numerous collections of Indian tales. The ones I most admire are those compiled by Alice Marriott and Carol K. Rachlin, those by Stith Thompson, and also those of George Bird Grinnell. Therefore most of the references in the list of sources are to these authors, rather than to other sources in which very similar versions appear.

In one case, the Upper Cowlitz story of Coyote which appears in Melville Jacobs's *Northwest Sahaptin Texts,* I have reprinted that version complete—since the original text is short and it perfectly demonstrates the kind of language which results from direct transcription of oral literature and gives a good basis for seeing what I have done with the story in my version.

These stories are not the property of any author but belong to an entire people. The Santee Dakota Charles Eastman wrote about his own Indian boyhood:

> Very early, the Indian boy assumed the task of preserving and transmitting the legends of his ancestors and his race. Almost every evening a myth or a true story of some deed done in the past was narrated by one of the parents or grandparents while the boy listened with parted lips and glistening eyes. On the following evening he was usually required to repeat it. If he was not an apt scholar, he struggled along with his task, but as a rule the Indian boy is a good listener and has a good memory so that the stories were tolerably well mastered. The household became his audience by which he was alternately criticized and applauded.

The odyssey of Anpao simply shapes this ancient task of preserving and transmitting Indian stories in order to offer them to a new and wider audience.

When I had completed *Anpao* and it was read by several elder Indian friends, they asked me if I thought that many white men would be able to grasp what I had written. I thought about the question for a long time and then decided that the message of *Anpao* is not as obscure as it might have been in the days of Columbus, Cortez, and Andrew Jackson —those invaders of the Indian world who considered the people they encountered to be less than human. The world has changed and we have come around to a viewpoint which for the first time in history sees a fundamental reality in the Indian concept of nature and of man's place in the cosmos. It seems to me that, of the many meanings conveyed by the stories in *Anpao,* the one which is surely the most central verifies a statement by Paul Radin, one of the foremost students of American Indian religion, which throws much light on *Anpao* and on Indians in general: "The Indian does not make the separation into personal as contrasted with impersonal in our sense at all. What he seems to be interested in is the whole question of existence, of reality; and everything that is perceived by the sense, thought of, felt, and dreamt of, exists for him."

That statement is a clear expression of the "wholeness" which is the central idea of American Indians and probably the single concept most difficult to convey to non-Indians. But the world is changing quickly and attitudes toward reality are far wider now than they were at any other time in history. Many of us are prepared to sail to strange places in time and in space; perhaps *Anpao* will address itself to that audience and become a personal journey for readers who wish to sail from one world to another.

Jamake Highwater
Missoula, Montana
1977

Notes on Sources

Page 13. "Ah, I Shall Tell" is the beginning of a Kiowa story from which the last tale in this book, "The Village Beneath the Water," is also taken (Marriott and Rachlin, 1968).

Page 15. "In the Days of the Plentiful" takes its main theme from the Blackfeet story of Scarface (Grinnell). This is the central, connective theme of *Anpao*. The name Ko-ko-mik-e-is is Blackfeet for "Night-red-light," which relates to the Moon. Anpao's eventual marriage to a Moon person emphasizes the union of Sun, Moon, and Earth which is the climax of the book.

Page 23. "The Magic of the Moon" also comes from the Blackfeet story of Scarface (Grinnell). The "Contrary" is a Plains Indian conception—a person who does and says everything backward during ceremonial days or when he is on a spiritual quest. This idea of persons who are divinely "contrary" is also found among the Southwest tribes in the form of ceremonial or sacred clowns who have complete license during ceremonies to do and say whatever they wish. The Clown/Contrary is exceedingly important to Indian sensibility for reasons too complex to summarize here. An excellent discussion of this figure appears in Tedlock. The poem "This prayer I offer you" comes from the Zuni song "Presenting an Infant to the Sun." The poem "My mother bore me" is a song from the Quechua.

Page 47. "The Dawn of the World" comes from both Blackfeet and Cheyenne sources. The Cheyenne story of how the world was made (Marriott and Rachlin, 1968) is very famous in the Southern Plains. The story of Old Man (or Napi) is Blackfeet; a version of it appears in Grinnell. The idea of the death of the creator is always shocking to non-Indians. There is a good discussion of this concept and how it generally affects Indian philosophy in Underhill (page 34). The name Anpao is the Dakota word for dawn.

Page 58. "Anpao Is Born" continues the story of Old Man (Napi), which also includes the segment on the reason people die (Grinnell). A famous Kiowa story tells about the woman who married the Sun and tried to return to her own people, and also about Grandmother Spider and the splitting of the boy into the half-boys (Marriott and Rachlin, 1968).

Page 79. "All That Happened Must Happen Again" returns to the Scarface story (Grinnell).

Page 87. "The Sky Beings" is Iroquoian (Marriott and Rachlin, 1968). The dream song, "Where the mountain crosses," is from the Papago Indians.

Page 102. "Snake Boy" is a Cheyenne story (Marriott and Rachlin, 1968).

Page 113. "The Sorceress" is a tale that is told at most modern powwows and intertribals; the story seems to have originated in the Oklahoma territory.

Page 125. "Anpao and the Animals" is found in Russell. The song "In the night" comes from the Papago Indians.

Page 140. "Anpao Brings the Corn" is a famous Zuni story (Marriott and Rachlin, 1968).

Page 151. "Anpao and Coyote" comes from the Sahaptian

Indians; it was collected and originally translated by Jacobs. The original text appears below for comparison with my rendering of this humorous tale. The humor of Indians has been greatly neglected, in part because of language and images that are tabooed by Judeo-Christian morality. Indians do not share the white man's views on profanity and decency. Whereas white men have jokes for private situations, as opposed to jokes for public ones, Indians have only one morality, which governs both private and public life. Now that the white world has come around to being open about language and humor which it once pretended did not exist, ribald humor of the sort that flourished in Chaucer, Boccaccio, and other early writers has returned to the white man's literature, providing a basis for understanding the audacious aspects of Indian humor.

Coyote borrows Break Wind's anus . . .

1. When Coyote was traveling, he encountered Break Wind boy. Break Wind boy had arrow in hand, target in hand. When he threw the target, p̓u″. Break Wind boy broke wind, the boy did so when he shot at it. (2) p̓u″, five arrows he had, p̓u″ he shot them at the target, when he had shot at and hit it with the five arrows, he would go on. p̓u′p̓u′p̓u′p̓u′p̓u′p̓u′p̓u″. He stooped, p̓u″, he threw it, p̓u″, he shot at it, p̓u″, all five arrows he shot at it.

2. When Coyote met him, he said to him, "Your thing is fine for a gathering of people. Give it to me."—"Why no. I want mine myself." He told him, at a move, it made p̓u″. (2) "But do give it to me now." He pleaded for it. "I'll give it to you then,"

he said to him. The breaking of wind was making the boy tired now, (so) he gave it all to Coyote, bow, arrows, target.

3. He said to him, "Come now, throw it!" Coyote threw it, p̓u". "Come now, shoot at it!" he said to him. Coyote shot at it, p̓u', all five arrows, and, p̓u'-p̓u'p̓u'. (2) The boy said to Coyote, "Go along now!" Coyote went, p̓u'p̓u'p̓u'. "Now I am going away," the boy told him. The boy ran on, he ran away as fast as he could.

4. When Coyote made a move, p̓u', he threw it, p̓u', he shot at it, p̓u', all five arrows, p̓u'p̓u'p̓u'p̓u'-p̓u'. When he went on, p̓u'p̓u'p̓u'p̓u'p̓u'p̓u'p̓u'. In no long time his rectum became sore. (2) Now, prrrrrrrrrr (rapid explosions), and then Coyote ran on in the same direction the boy had run. He followed him, p̓u'p̓u'p̓u', he called to him, "Where are you? (3) I want to return your breaking of wind to you again." Though he shouted and shouted, the boy did not answer. Coyote now felt very ill with his rectum. He remained absolutely still, (but) when he moved, prrrrrrrr.

5. He lay down, and he thought, "I will defecate and have it figured out." (2) He had two younger sisters, the sisters were Pine Nut and Huckleberry. He defecated them. "Now then! You will explain, my younger sisters, how I have become like this."—(3) "Think it out yourself now! You will say, 'That is just how I had been forgetting!' "—"t̓ᵘt̓ᵘt̓ᵘ, tell! tell! tell!"—"Be careful! older brother! be careful!

older brother!" (4) That is how Coyote asked for [threatened] rain. "That powerful boy is Break Wind. You should throw away bow, arrows and target there." (5) "That is just what I had been forgetting, my two younger sisters." When he threw them away, he went on, without breaking wind.

Page 159. "Deer Woman" is a modern story of the Ponca and other Oklahoma tribes, essentially to explain prostitution among the young women who vanish at powwows and, as far as the story is concerned, go off to the cities and become prostitutes (Marriott and Rachlin, 1968).

Page 168. "The Drowned Boys" is a Cheyenne story which is also told by the Southern Utes (Marriott and Rachlin, 1968).

Page 183. "The Sun Journey" returns to the Blackfeet story of Scarface (Grinnell).

Page 194. "Anpao and the Magic Dogs" is taken from a variety of sources and includes direct quotations of dialogue and actions recorded in early journals. Most of the reports are found in the journals of the Coronado expedition of the Southwest; others are from Ewers. Direct quotations from Indian speeches and oral tradition are from Hamilton. The story of the "fireboat-walks-on-mountains" is taken from Eastman. The image of the bearded invader looking like a dog with a squirrel in his mouth comes from Chief Kahkewquonaby. Most of the stories of the first horses and the first rifles to find their way into Indian hands are from Ewers.

Page 206. "The Battle with the Birds" is also from the Blackfeet tale of Scarface (Grinnell).

Page 216. "He Comes from the East" is a famous Kiowa

story that is told in Oklahoma as part of a cycle of tales of the trickster Saynday. There are many tales dealing with the coming of smallpox (Marriott and Rachlin, 1968).

Page 227. "The Village Beneath the Water" returns to the Kiowa story from which "Ah, I Shall Tell" is taken (Marriott and Rachlin, 1968). This Kiowa story of the underwater village is interwoven with the end of the Blackfeet tale of Scarface (Grinnell). The concluding poem comes from the Ghost Dance of the Paiute and the Comanche. The Ghost Dance religion was the climax of revivalist movements among Indians who feared spiritual bankruptcy in the wake of the white man's invasion. They grasped desperately at religious cults that prophesied the defeat of the invaders and the ultimate spiritual victory of Indians. The Ghost Dance originated in 1870 among the Northern Paiute who lived on the California-Nevada border. The first transcontinental run on the Union Pacific railroad had recently been completed and no doubt inspired the vision of the Indian prophet Wodziwob: A great train would bring back his dead ancestors and all the buffaloes and would announce its arrival with an immense explosion—perhaps inspired by the explosives used by the railroad builders and by the gushes of steam and noise that the train's engines produced.

Bibliography

Bierhorst, John. *In the Trail of the Wind: American Indian Poems and Ritual Orations.* New York: Dell Publishing Co., 1971.

Eastman, Charles A. (Ohiyesa). *Indian Boyhood.* New York: Fawcett World Library, 1976.

Ewers, John C. *The Blackfeet.* Norman, Okla.: University of Oklahoma Press, 1958.

Farb, Peter. *Man's Rise to Civilization: As Shown by the Indians of North America.* New York: E. P. Dutton & Co., 1968.

Grinnell, George Bird. *Blackfoot Lodge Tales.* Lincoln, Nebr.: University of Nebraska Press, 1962.

Hamilton, Charles. *Cry of the Thunderbird: An American Indian's Own Story.* Norman, Okla.: University of Oklahoma Press, 1972.

Jacobs, Melville, trans. and ed. *Northwest Sahaptin Texts.* New York: Columbia University Press, 1934.

Marriott, Alice, and Rachlin, Carol K. *American Indian Mythology.* New York: New American Library, 1968.

————. *Plains Indian Mythology.* New York: Thomas Y. Crowell Co., 1975.

Russell, Frank. "Myths of the Jicarilla Apache," *Journal of American Folklore* XI, no. 11 (1939).

Tedlock, Dennis, and Tedlock, Barbara, eds. *Teachings from the American Earth*. New York: Liveright, 1975.

Thompson, Stith. *Tales of the North American Indians*. Bloomington, Ind.: Indiana University Press, 1972.

Underhill, Ruth M. *Red Man's Religion*. Chicago: University of Chicago Press, 1965.

JAMAKE HIGHWATER's *Anpao: An American Indian Odyssey* won the 1978 Newbery Honor Award, the Boston Globe/Horn Book Honor Award, and the ALA Best Book for Young Adults Award. He is also the author of *Many Smokes, Many Moons*, an American Indian chronology, which won the Jane Addams Peace Book Award for 1979; *The Sun, He Dies*, a novel about the end of the Aztec world; *Song from the Earth: North American Indian Painting*, winner of the 1981 Anisfield-Wolf Award; *The Sweet Grass Lives On: Fifty Contemporary North American Indian Artists; Moonsong Lullaby; Dance: Rituals of Experience*; the three volumes in the Ghost Horse cycle: *Legend Days*, a 1985 Jefferson Cup Award Honor Book (Virginia Library Association), a 1984 ALA Best Books for Young Adults and *School Library Journal* Best Book; *The Ceremony of Innocence*, a 1985 ALA Best Book for Young Adults; and *I Wear the Morning Star*, as well as *The Primal Mind*, which is the basis of a PBS television documentary. He has also written many reviews and articles for major magazines and journals.

FRITZ SCHOLDER, of Luiseno Indian extraction, is known internationally for his revolutionary paintings and lithographs of the Native American.

The four lithographs from stone for ANPAO represent the first time he has collaborated with an author to illustrate a book. Of them he says, "The lithographs were done with the narrative fresh in my mind. The images are not literal, for that is the purpose of the text. For me, the owl, the buffalo, the bat, and death are mysterious and magical subjects."